A Will of His Own

Reflections

on Parenting

a Child

with Autism

Kelly Harland

Woodbine House   2002

All rights reserved. Published in the United States of America by Woodbine House, Inc., 6510 Bells Mill Road, Bethesda, MD 20817. 800-843-7323. http://www.woodbinehouse.com

"William" from *White Pine: Poems and Prose Poems* by Mary Oliver, copyright 1994 by *Poetry,* reprinted by permission of Harcourt, Inc.

Library of Congress Cataloging-in-Publication Data

Harland, Kelly.
   A will of his own : reflections on parenting a child with autism / by Kelly Harland.—1st ed.
      p. cm.
   ISBN 1-890627-19-4 (pbk.)
   1.Autism in children. 2. Autistic children—Care. 3. Autistic children—Family relationships. 4. Parenting. 5. Child rearing. I. Title.

RJ506.A9 H268 2002
618.92'8982—dc21   2002023491

Manufactured in the United States of America

First edition
10 9 8 7 6 5 4 3 2 1

A
Will
of
His
Own

*F*or Pat Close

Patti Corcoran

and RinaMarie Leon-Guerrero

Now there's William. He comes pecking, like a bird, at my heart. His eyebrows are like the feathers of a wren. His ears are little seashells.

I would keep him always in my mind's eye.

Soon enough he'll be tall, walking and conversing; he'll have ideas, and a capricious will; the passions will unfold in him, like greased wheels, and he will leap forward upon them.

Who knows, maybe he'll be an athlete, quick and luminous; or a musician, bent like a long-legged pin over the piano's open wing; or maybe he will stand day after day over a draftsman's desk, making something exquisite and useful—a tower or a bridge.

Whatever he does, he'll want the world to do it in. Maybe, who knows, he'll want this very room which, only for convenience, I realize, I've been calling mine.

I feel myself begin to wilt, like an old flower, weak in the stem.

But he is irresistible! Whatever he wants of mine—my room, my ideas, my glass of milk, my socks and shirts, my place in line, my portion, my world—he may have it.

— "William," by Mary Oliver

$\mathcal{T}$able of Contents

$\mathcal{I}$ntroduction

"Life would be nothing without her." My friend Jane, a single mom, was writing to me about her daughter. The statement struck me where I live. I thought it said everything there is to be said about being a mother.

I definitely know: my life now would be nothing without Will. It was a great life before he burst into it, but now it is richer. My life is full of discovery and deep indescribable pain and ridiculously out-of-control elation, all on account of this little boy.

If you are a parent with a child moving forward and up on the "typical" scale of development, then you know most of the same feelings. If you are raising a boy or girl like mine, whose chart looks different, who presents extreme and often insurmountable challenges, then you know that some of the feelings go deeper—that they can blow through your heart with the force of a stronger, chillier wind. You've known heartbreak. Yet as a mother or father, you may have metamorphosed into the person-of-all-hats you never thought you'd become:

researcher, therapist, skilled communicator, legal expert, enlightened humanitarian.

I have my dark times, when I'm almost overcome by the challenges that face me. And of course I long for an easier life for my child, and dream of a day when we won't have to fight so hard. But the way I view myself since Will is mainly in a powerful, positive light. It seems I was a shallow well before. Now my life's horizon has been stretched, it's longer, it gives me so much more room to explore. The sun comes up every morning on this line of my life, puzzling and perfect—and yes, painful—all at once, but aglow with hope, simply because of my son and the amazing boy he has turned out to be.

In my celebration of one little boy and his persona, I am really giving only a small glimpse into the world of autism. (And this collection of essays does turn out to be a celebration, for even though I've recorded moments of our family's trials, Will's exuberant spirit invaded every page without my even being aware of it, and prevented those emotions from dominating.) Autism Spectrum Disorder, as many doctors and parents in the community now prefer to call it, manifests itself in so many ways, and is often misunderstood because each child or adult, in spite of having similar symptoms, can exhibit such individual characteristics. My husband and I are extraordinarily blessed that our son is verbal. And in spite of his difficulty in meeting new people, he has always been, at various times, capable of giving out huge amounts of affection, especially to his ever-grateful mom. Still, his social and learning disabilities are profound. Other children may have better reading skills, or may not experience some of the anxiety Will is forced to deal with. There are children with severe challenges, and there are high-functioning junior NASA scientists. There are so many levels, so many differences across the spectrum, and there are, by now, a variety of techniques and strategies and medications to help, and even change, kids with autism. There may be, somewhere out there, a miracle.

But the pages I've written in the early dawn, while my family sleeps and before the small swashbuckler leaps out of bed and comes to take me on our day's voyage, are not really about all the things pertaining to autism, that insidious disorder that no one can seem to get a handle on. Though I have researched it extensively, I barely feel qualified to speak on the subject; the title of this book could just as easily be "Reflections on Parenting a Child"—with the last two words of the subtitle left off. For these sketches of my life with my son are about navigating Will's universe, about mapping the world he has pulled me into, with his love, his courage, and his gifted, mysterious ways. The diagnostic A-word, whatever its meaning, so often does not apply.

I couldn't have sketched my stories, or lived them in the hope-filled way I have, without the help of many people: especially Wendy McCulloch, Barbara Benson, Rena d'Adolf, and Rachel Paul; Jennifer Annable, Lisa Batkoff, Jodi Minkin, Misty Woods, Nel Taylor, Christi Clark, Janice Murphy, Claudia Allan, and Rosemary Washington; my friends Jane Ann Warner, Kathy Bylenok, Betsy Fay, Victoria Lauber, Jane Peck, Ann Wicker, Sue Loppnow, Midge Lanphere, Julie Dalke, Ann McKee, Cleo Delaney, Petie Morley, and Libby Torrance; Patricia de la Bretonne (who gave me the poem "William" by Mary Oliver); John Keegan; Daniel Gottkin; Irv Shapell, Fran Marinaccio, and Brenda Ruby of Woodbine House; Beth Kephart; and certainly other parents, teachers and friends I haven't named who've been right beside Will and his father and me on our journey. I never knew there could be so much kindness in the world.

Thanks to my editor, Susan Stokes, who championed my essays from the beginning and who has helped to guide me down this sometimes difficult and always amazing path of writing.

And to my remarkable husband, my pure everlasting gratefulness and love.

Kelly Harland
June 2002

Now

Moonlight

This is where we are now.

It's an early September evening and Will and I are sitting on a wooden bench beneath a crescent moon. The sky is black, the air is crisp and cool with the onset of autumn, and high up in the dark the bright moon, hung at an angle, burns silver. We rest with our arms touching before a big fountain, the one that seemed such an unusual structure when it was first unveiled in the center of our upscale neighborhood shopping center a couple of years ago. It was designed to stand as an oasis amidst the buzzing palatial stores and quaint cafes that surround it, and now here it looms, a mini-Stonehenge-with-waterfalls, lit up like an attraction in the twilight. Will and I have learned to appreciate it, because the kids can actually play in it in summer, and on a night like tonight it soothes—it sings, as water spurts abundantly from the top of the big stones and splashes into the shining pool at their base.

Now the merchants are getting ready to lock their doors: we have already spent an hour or so inside the shops, not shopping, never shopping, but running all around as we always do, mother chasing boy, boy bumping into other boys who are picking out pencils in the school supplies section of the drugstore, boys chattering away about which color notebook to buy, on this eve of the week before my boy's third grade life begins. William simply cannot stand still in a school supplies aisle, or in any other section of any place of business. He bounces off the walls, he "sharks" as his occupational therapist calls it—runs the inside perimeter of the building, moving round and round and round at rapid speed. There is too much stuff in a store, too much for his brain to handle, so the aisles are enough—the aisles and the doors and the exit signs are what he sees and knows, the things that guide him through the chaos.

That race through stores, which began when Will was two (he is now ten), has become just a regular part of our lives, like a stroll in the park. So our dip into the drugstore lasts a total of three or four minutes, and the same for all the other stores in the village of shops. Then finally, here on the bench by the shimmering fountain, the chase is over and the little shark relaxes. We are in the open air, in the calm night, and there is nothing to stimulate but cascading water and its burbling melody. We are alone in the moonlight.

The conversation, led by him, goes like this:

"Elementary school has fourth grade and fifth grade left to go." His green eyes stare up at Stonehenge, reflecting silver light, flashing with thoughts.

"Yes," I say.

"After that, we don't know what middle school I'm going to choose."

"Right." He once drew a chart on his chalkboard of all the grades up through four years of college. Then he added: "Job—2 years."

"It could be Hamilton, or Eckstein." Will knows every last school building in the Seattle district. He's made his father and me drive past each one of them a hundred times. We've traipsed them on foot during off-hours and we know every corner and cranny. It is the layout of each school campus that pulls him—the halls, the boys' and girls' bathrooms. Little variations on a design that is, when set apart from bustling hollering crowds of students, so beautifully predictable.

"Could be." I'm really listening now, after doing our store-run on automatic pilot.

"Could be," Will echoes. My heart is brought up short . If there happened to be anyone passing by, this little boy's manner of speaking would sound odd. It comes out in a funny sing-song, so baby-like for a child his size. And the mother's voice in response might sound casual, like a normal mom talking to her kid. But in true matter of fact, the kid is at his shining, unprecedented best and Mom is holding her breath. I am, as my soul starts to stir, trying to contain myself. This is a *conversation*. This is something that has been an incredible uphill battle for Will—something that we work hard, every day, to achieve. For years we've paid professionals to assist us with this. We've written stories about it to try to get it going. And now here it is, rolling along spectacularly, without struggle, the words sailing happily up into the luxuriant night air.

"After high school comes college." This is a new one on me. "Yes, college." I say. "Maybe," I add quickly.

"I'll go to the University of Washington. I'll have my lunch in the Student Union building. I'll have a cookie, a muffin, or a scone."

Now I feel the need to interject and not for reasons of nutrition. "People have to pay a lot of money to go there, you know, Will. Lots of people are trying to get in. We'll see." Why can't I just let him dream on, a child's dream? It's because I know. He gets these things in his mind and he is like no child or human I have ever seen. The thought forms in concrete and can't be moved. Once built, it stays and stays—till he graduates from high school and he's standing there confronting me as if no time had ever lapsed between this moment and the future. He'll be asking me then about the UW, I'm sure of it. But now the fall night crackles and he goes on—disregarding my warning, and to my utter amazement.

"After that I'll get a job. I'll live in an apartment down by the waterfront. I'll work at the Seattle Trade Center. I'll ride my bike."

Excellent! My concerns over how I'll create a private class-room at the UW vanish. I'm delighted with this design for a career track. I'm especially pleased that there is no car on it.

"I think there's a bike rack at the Trade Center," he says. Yes, as a matter of fact, there probably is. "I'll have an office. . . and a computer. . . and a view of the railroad tracks!" Certainly. Now the scent of some faraway harvest-night bonfire rides past me on the breeze and I am caught up. I snuggle into my sweater. This exchange is a miracle. I'm hearing about a dream—a dream!—from a boy whose way of thinking is so narrow and delayed it doesn't seem possible that a dream would be allowed in. And I'm imagining: the Trade Center. Can't one rent office space there? Couldn't I set something up?

"Maybe you'll even have an office door with your name on it!"

He scoots to the edge of the bench. "I'll have a sign that says: 'Will!'"

Everything in the shopping center is turned off, but the water in the fountain is still at play, tumbling and splashing in the spotlight, echoing Will's cry. So many nights I have lain awake as tears-mixed-with-prayers dampened my pillow. I've put in a lot of time in the dark, feeling heavy and helpless and terrified for a future I can't predict. But all of a sudden the future has revealed itself from the other side, and it's being held up before my eyes like an Olympic torch. Whatever has led us to this—years of speech therapy, hours upon hours of my own in-put based on instinct and a few educated guesses, his father's incredible talent for showing him a way to walk through this world—William can see his dream, and it looks good. In fact, it looks perfect. And he's telling me all about it.

The Shock of the New

We'd had a few weeks without a problem. I was beginning to take for granted the fact that we could move through a morning, an afternoon, perhaps even a whole day without a flip-out or a freak-out. Sometimes, in my indefatigable optimism, I get to a place where I really believe the whole nightmare is over—the nightmare that consists of watching the littlest thing suddenly send my child into tears and frantic helplessness. I actually start to relax, like someone whose sailboat is floating peacefully after being buffeted around by a storm. But something eventually comes up again, out of the blue, in a flash, an electrifying bolt.

This time it was those little sticks that divide up the groceries on the supermarket conveyor belt. I don't think the regular population notices them much—I don't even know what they're officially called. You pick them up, you set them between your purchases and the next guy's, you don't think twice about them. You've probably never noticed that they usually have the store logo on them. I know that I had never even looked at how many are grouped together beside the cash register until that day.

Will had never noticed the dividers before either, but on this day he did, and since he was seeing them for the first time, they threw him for a loop. They changed what was happening in his predictable check-out routine—push cart through, ring up purchases, pay money, go out to car. Something was different, and it surprised him.

I try to explain to people what "different" and "surprise" can do to our family, but I don't think it can be explained. Because when the moment strikes, when the fear comes over Will's face, when he throws the sticks and takes off and you run after him with the startled faces of shoppers in your mental rearview mirror, when he gets in the car and bursts into hysterical tears and you put your hand over his heart and it's running at 150 beats a minute—well, life takes on a bizarre quality. Did a two-ton monster breathing flames pop up next to the grocery clerk? If only it were true—if it could be something that easy, something a shield and a spear could fix. No, to save the day in these situations—when your child is hyperventilating and turning ashen because he glimpsed a grocery store divider stick—you must wear a more ingenious kind of armor.

This happened on a perfectly glorious Seattle day, when we had been driving around in the sun, crossing our favorite city bridges and stopping off at parks and little bakeries and feeling like nothing could stop us. Then the day was ruined. Sometimes a bridge ruins the day—by sounding a clanging bell, stopping traffic, and opening up for a boat to go through (this can be really bad). Sometimes the park ruins it—by sporting a section of new grass that is cordoned off by yellow tape. Sometimes the bakery is the culprit—normally they're open but today there is a "Closed" sign in the window. "Open" and "Closed" signs can affect Will's mood in the most significant way.

And though I've toughened, I mostly ride around on a roller coaster when it comes to these things. I panic, I groan, if I happen to be out on my own and I see a banner proclaiming "Going Out of Business" on one of Will's favorite stores. (A shop gets added to our "Favorites" list by virtue of the design of the sign over its door, or because of the doors themselves or the layout of the aisles—never because of the merchandise contained inside.) I know I must start working on a plan to break the news to William, who will be—well, devastated would not be too strong a word. He'll be crushed, and it will take him awhile, maybe weeks, to get over a loss that isn't at all sentimental. His feelings are based on something I can't fathom, the simple fact that something that was there, and that was there over and over again, is not there anymore.

His father and I have formed a little swat team. We will read a brief mention in our local newspaper of a corporate takeover—the "Pay-Rite" chain, it announces, will soon be sold and renamed "Buy More"—and to us the tiny headline stands out like a blaring billboard. Grateful for advance warning, the team immediately responds. When will we begin prepping our charge? How bad will it be? Chain store closures put us on the alert in the worst way. The store and its sign are the familiar, comforting landmarks that help our child find his way in the world. He lives for repetition, for sameness—it is a need that is built into him. My husband, Charles, and I know painfully well what is going to happen to all three of us when suddenly one day, in places all across the city, that big sign comes down.

Of the many things that affect our daily life—guiding our child through school, pressing him toward socialization, trying to expand his five-item food menu, finding ways to help him color a picture or glue pipe cleaners to construction paper when sensory overload and motor skill problems cause him to shy away from any kind of art work—it's our role as human buffers in the face of life's little changes that is the most difficult job Charles and I face, and the one that demands the most of us in terms of cleverness and cunning. There are tools. Early in Will's life we learned how to draw "social stories," little cartoon strips with stick figure boys doing the stuff every kid does, but mapped out in a straightforward way to explain the how and why. Since he locks onto a simple visual image, the cartoon strips can work like a charm. We've used these maps to assist us with everything from "How to Say Hello" to potty training. So now, if we are going to change something in a room in our house—let's say we are going to move in a new couch or are planning, believe it or not, to change a light fixture—we use them to stem the tide. It will take weeks of preparation to get him ready.

Here's how it begins. Day One: Will, I think I'm going to get a new comforter for my bed. Day Four: Will, I've found the comforter and it's coming sometime in May! In just a few weeks! Day Eight: We can't wait for our new bedding, can we? It will have blue flowers on it (by now I've purchased the fluffy intruder and it sits in the closet awaiting its debut). At last I whip out paper and pen. I draw an eight-panel story about Will discovering the new bed. "Something new is coming to my mom's bedroom," reads the caption underneath the first box, and the little stick figure Will has a question mark over his head. In the last box the stick kid jumps for joy. "It's okay!" reads the caption. "I'm getting used to changes! I like the new bed!" We read this every day for about two weeks straight.

It's a hit-and-miss operation. When we brought in a new sofa, everything worked great. But on the Day of the Comforter, Will threw a fit. He carried it out the back door and down our alley to a neighbor's recycling box hundreds of feet away. I retrieved it and gave it to one of my girlfriends.

Why does it happen? And why do things sometimes enter Will's life without a trace of shock or upset, allowing us a taste of what it would be like for Will to be "normal"? The autism that invades Will's entire person, that forces him to require concrete structure and repeating patterns in order to make sense of anything, can leave him in an extraordinarily vulnerable position if that structure is missing. Because of this, Will must feel threatened by many things, a lot of the time. His dad and I try to divide his scares into three categories: the small ones that dissipate in a minute or two; the ones that truly are traumatic; and the ones he uses to manipulate his parents, for yes, this bright little boy knows how quickly we run to his rescue when a moment from one of the first two categories arrives, and we are always trying to balance ourselves along that fine line.

Charles and I are constantly on the alert for signals, the way I imagine parents whose kids are allergic to certain foods do autopilot scans of snack tables at birthday parties. Often, like two soldier buddies in a trench, we anticipate the enemy and pull off a maneuver just in time. (Private Mom is preserved forever on one video, rushing to comfort Will because I know his party guests are about to sing "Happy Birthday," and I didn't forewarn him it was coming, and he is going to fall apart.) We do not do battle alone. Therapists have been on the case, and doctors, and anti-anxiety medication is now playing a role when all else fails. There is a lot of work, since this stuff comes up in its moderate form every day, and, as a straight-out-of-left-field electroshock, just about once a week.

The grocery store incident definitely rated as one of the electroshocks. In its aftermath, Will and I pulled ourselves together by talking about the divider sticks a lot, talking about why they upset him, and discussing why they are there and why we must get used to them. And now, when I go to the supermarket with him, I simply set my groceries on the conveyer belt far apart from the next guy's.

When I am in a toy store with Will and he never, never can allow me to buy him a toy—because to remove the item from the shelf (a change) would cause him distress—I have learned to firmly take hold of myself. Toys aren't everything, I force myself to think. I try not to hear the other little voices in the store pleading with their parents to buy them this and that. I try not to think about the fact that if I could, I would buy him the priciest toy in the store—I would buy him all the toys, if only he would let me. As Private Mom, of course, I go back to the store alone, pick out something surefire, and make a cartoon strip for it.

"I like things to be the same," Will often remarks proudly. It is his identity, and I am so grateful that he can express his feelings about himself. But it is the part of his identity that I want to see, and that I must believe I will see, change. The part that, when he tenses, when he runs, when he cries out in terror, I want to change into something utterly, drastically different.

Ferryboats

Along the Seattle wharf the noon sun lavishes gold light on brilliant blue water. Will and I are giggling and jogging all the way to the ferry dock, where the boats, white and proud with black-and-green trim, sit high overlooking the stairways and walkways of the busy terminal. As we hurry past the waterfront, the stately vessels get bigger, bigger. It is so exciting. All day long Will has been saying. "I'm finally hooked on ferryboats!"

Here is what he means: prior to this May day, in his young life, he has been hooked on escalators (mainly), elevators (a lot), exit signs, and the hand-dryers in public bathrooms. And as his little legs ran and danced toward and around and up and down these modern-day appliances, his parents followed. We had no other choice, it seemed. For William, a trip to the park to visit a four-dryer men's room seemed as fabulous as a visit to Disney World would seem to most other kids. We tried to talk him out of these obsessions, of course, and behavioral and occupational therapists worked to try to influence him in the same way, but no breakthrough came. So we gave our son his joy. We rode up and down a hundred escalators, and went to the aquarium so he could race past green sea life on his way to the green exit signs. We stood patiently as he pressed the magic button on automatic hand dryers from one end of the city to another. He'd wake up on a Saturday and crow, "Mama and Papa are going to take me to see blowers today!" Mama and Papa steeled themselves and looked around for a paperback novel to help them make it through the next "Blower Tour."

Friends say, "What patience!" A mother said to me, "What surrender!" It is true, I have surrendered, his father and I both have surrendered, our time, our hearts, our lives, our mental health. We've helped Will work hard in school, we've read to him, we've intervened at every opportunity to try to show him the treasures of life that do not necessarily go on and off, up and down. We would have taken him anywhere to get his mind off his fixations. But when it came time to play, well, we figured out the score—it was off to a skyscraper with forty-two floors.

But now we've made it to the ferry dock. We stand together staring up at our new obsession and I'm thinking that this— well, this could actually pass for normal. My boy loves boats! We can be here in the open air, in the sunshine. We can sniff the breeze of Puget Sound and, humbled by the size of the queenly ships, look up and study their uniform design. And naturally I know that's part of the attraction—they all look the same. I also know that they go back and forth, back and forth. But who cares? There is so much to ferry life, so many variations on the theme. Already today we have lingered at the entrance to the terminal where there hangs a series of sepia-toned photographs from the archives of Washington State. It tells the story of the early ferryboats. William stood still—stood still!—to study the prints. We are so beautifully far from being stuck in a whistling steel box, staring at numbers on a lighted panel!

Then comes the sound of the horn. "It's the Wenatchee!" cries Will, right on the money as he sees his boat slowly pulling out of the dock in all its glory, smokestack puffing. "And over there is the Hyak!" At home he will spend hours pretending he is a ferry (sometimes the captain and sometimes the boat) on its run, on all the routes from Seattle to the San Juan Islands. He recites the safety announcement again and again: "Smoking is only allowed on the upper deck—smoking is not allowed in the passenger cabin." He likes to cast me as the ticket taker. He builds models of each ferry out of Legos. He draws overhead maps of the boats. He keeps a collection of Northwest postcards depicting each one. He likes to say, "Mama, which one is your favorite?" I choose a favorite. I do not tell him that they all look the same to me.

Then, of course, the best part of all. We can ride them! We can take trips! My kid is beginning to understand that a reward may be waiting at the end. A park, a little street of tourist shops. He can find something of interest in these things, as long as he knows he'll be riding the boat. His grandmother's house is across the water. For a boy who is reluctant to try anything new, this magic fleet of carriers can help to widen his world.

The adventures do not come without a hitch. Once Will was scared out of his wits by a loud boat horn, so he now insists on wearing protective headphones on every trip. He can be ambushed by an excruciating anxiety attack if things aren't "the same"—if a particular boat on a particular run has been changed, or if the announcement that comes over the loudspeaker is different. (I try to explain to him that there are miscellaneous guys and gals improvising up there on the microphone, even though sometimes during one of his attacks I wish I'd gone up to the pilot house with a script.) Going on the boats is not like watching them move in and out of their places from afar. It is entering the real-life world of travel where anything can happen—a sometimes nerve-wracked, love-hate experience that confounds the whole family. But we have determined that it is somehow worth whatever we have to go through.

Last summer, the first summer of the ferryboat, we went to a city park to play in a big local wading pool, crowded with kids. Before I knew it, Will had splashed his way out to the middle of the pond, where I could barely see him but could hear him chanting, oblivious to everyone and everything: "Now arriving, San Juan Island!" He was thrilled to have real water for his game, and I relaxed on the bank, knowing that this would keep him occupied for awhile. But trouble arrived in the form of a lifeguard's whistle. A buff blond boy was clearing the pool, calling, "Everybody out for twenty minutes! Twenty minutes!" He was about to throw some cleaning solvent around, but what he didn't know and I knew was that my kid was not going to budge. He was in the middle of his boat game and there would be no interruption without an enormous noisy battle involving all three of us.

I hopped in the water but I was many feet away from Will, calling out in complete and utter futility for him to come to me. The lifeguard, red-faced, was angrily scattering his crystals. "Get out, kid!" he yelled. "Get out of the pool right now!" The audience of families sat watching on the green banks, frozen like the pointillist figures of Seurrat. The hushed silence was broken by only one thing—the official announcement that came blaring from one little boy who was way out in the water, who was slowly and steadily raising one arm up in the air as if it were a crossing gate: "Now arriving, Bainbridge Island. Passengers please return to your vehicles now. Passengers: please enjoy your trip!"

He was one with his boat and there was nothing that could possibly mobilize him. No one on the real-world shore got it. They gaped at his mysterious performance. But I got it. And the tiny twinge of anxiety I felt as I again witnessed Will's expertise at finding ways to remove himself from the rest of humanity was nothing compared to how I felt in seeing his bliss at having an enormous pond to himself for his ferries. He stretched his arm up to the summer sky, lifting the imaginary gate. Deep down I know, when he honks his horn and revs up his engines, that we have actually come a step further. That a boat can show us the sea and the sea can introduce us to sea life, and maybe this is how we will be able to approach nature, and adventure, and science. And surely there must be other people interested in ferryboats. Slowly, over time, we will be able to use all this. The obsession will help us break through—I won't let it hold us back. He is fixated and it is abnormal, but although this may appear to be a window that is slammed shut, there is a crack where the light comes in—that just like any child who plays in an imaginary world Will is also in love.

The summer lifeguard gave up and worked around the ferryboat and the pond got its cleaning. A hundred kids jumped back in laughing and splashing and playing their own games, and the exceptional little boy blended right into the crowd again.

And now at the real dock a few seasons later, Will studies the carved wooden sign on the front of the boat that has just come in, the Kitsap. I watch the silver-white gulls hovering at the helm. They float and dip like little mascots, guiding the grand ferry into port. "Mom, is the Kitsap your favorite?" Will asks. A red-and-white gate rises and a ferry worker signals the cars to drive off. "They're all my favorites, honey," I tell him.

Potter vs. Potter

When I started my volunteer job working in the school library, on Wednesdays in the afternoon, I found myself handling the books as if they were treasures, holding each one like a coveted gift before I pushed it into its place on the shelf. Every now and then I'd glance around at the room with its walls of books and tall windows and feel a glow in my heart. I was a legitimate, bona fide elementary school mom.

Two years ago I'd been feeling rather helpless about Will's education. I believed we'd have to enroll him in a private school in order to get him the attention he required, but Will's dad and I went to look at many of those schools, the best, most expensive ones in Seattle, and none of them seemed to be equipped to handle all the stuff we'd be bringing with us. In the public schools, we found "special" classes, separated from the regular rooms, but we went to observe them and quickly knew that our son needed to be in a setting with typically developing kids, the way he had been in preschool. Finally we found Montlake, a public school not far from our neighborhood, an "inclusion model." We interviewed the Special Ed team there and found them very much to our liking. Of course, once we'd discovered this promising place we had to turn into political foxes, and audition like crazy to get in. But we were accepted. And things had gone okay. Will had, with much professional assistance, gotten all the way to the third grade in classes with regular children, where he often had an excruciating time keeping up. But, as usual, he rode high on his remarkable spirit and made it through.

I think back to the day I returned from the pediatrician's office, during the second year of Will's life, after the doctor had dropped the devastating news of his condition. The world was black, my beautiful little home with its pastel Peter Rabbit nursery and bright plastic toys strewn all over the floor seemed black, my whole life had changed during the course of a routine doctor visit. It was one of those visits that is supposed to mark your child's development, put him in a percentile bracket: the regular six-month "Healthy Child" meeting after which you feel fairly satisfied and go off with your baby to the park and play.

But the second the doctor's eyes met mine I felt the foundation of my life fall away. She had used the word "delayed" and when Charles and I came back to our house with me still trembling, I handed my baby boy his bottle, touched his curls with a brand-new tenderness, and went to my desk. I looked up "delay" in the dictionary, because I wanted the word to bail me out of all this. I wanted it to say, "A passing phase in development, applied to a mental condition and lasting only a short time." But it was not to be. Near the dictionary on my desk I noticed a newspaper catalog of schools I'd been perusing just the day before, still open to the page showing descriptions of some of our local private academies, with many of the names highlighted in yellow pen. Like all the parent overachievers I knew, I had been panicking, thinking we had to get on waiting lists right away, even though Will was only a little over two years old. For our only child, only the best would do.

But with the storm of information that was suddenly batting my mind around in what seemed like a whole new landscape, I was forced to make adjustment after adjustment in my thinking. I was being swept along a fast track. All my life I had looked upon the little universe of people with disabilities from my privileged window seat, but now I was being ejected from my spot and thrown right into the middle of it. When, after a couple of months, things at last settled down—after I'd written a hundred tear-stained pages in my journal, read everything there was to read on the subject of autism, spoken at length with professionals, and begun networking with mothers of little ones like mine—the sky cleared a bit and I saw what I was left with, what I had. A special boy, a wonderful boy. And a purpose in life. As a parent I had already figured out that I was going to have to try to be a teacher, but now I would need to hone my skills in a way I'd never imagined. A new strength pumped through my system like a steroid injection. After the grieving evolved into a new awareness, this power bestowed itself upon me like the sun. No matter what hardships came my way, I knew I'd be up to the task.

Yet along the journey there was always reason to keep a stiff upper lip, always a moment when I found myself forced to pluck up a certain amount of courage. Here in the Montlake Library this spring, it was Harry Potter. The Harry Potter books were sweeping the nation, the whole world. The kids in Will's class were devouring them. But Will's reading, his narrow interests, and his developmental "delay" created a giant impenetrable wall between his world and the world of J. K. Rowling. People who didn't know us that well seemed to be constantly asking me, "How does Will like Harry Potter?" and I wanted to say, "Will loves Pooh, Will loves Arthur and the characters from Sesame Street! Will adores the world of children's books! Does that work okay?"

On this particular Wednesday, as I filed away a couple of copies of *Charlotte's Web* and sorted through a stack of books on Egypt, I listened to two other volunteer mothers and the librarian discuss the new Harry Potter book that was to be released that summer. They mentioned characters from the previous stories, and brought up magical words and names I'd never heard before. "I'll bet Abigail just can't wait for the new one," said the librarian to one of the moms. "Is she excited?" The mother laughed. "What kid in third grade isn't?" she replied.

I thought I was beyond lumps in my throat, but I guess I wasn't yet. I thought I was beyond feeling the heavy heart of an outsider after glowing like a smug insider, and I was fairly sure I was beyond the envy, the longing. But this sort of thing still came up all the time, really. What was my kid not doing that all the other kids were? Well, most things. You've *got* to take him to see such and such movie, someone would say about the latest kiddie flick. But Will can't process the information that rushes past him on the silver screen. The movie theatre experience confuses him. Has he yet been to see a baseball game or any type of sports event? No. We drive by the big stadium all the time and he loves to see it, but once when we went past, he got a glimpse of the roaring crowd. That was enough for Will. A game, people, crowds, noise, chaos. Hot dogs, alien food, smells, sounds that come out of the blue. No spectator sports yet. Videos? A few. But since he doesn't know what might come at him when the tape starts rolling, he nixes most titles most of the time.

And then, the reading issue. He certainly hasn't progressed as far as his classmates and does all his reading for class separately from them. The work he is given is tailored to his needs and his school does a wonderful job of helping him. I try to remember not to compare, just like all parents who tell themselves everything will come in good time. At moments I ache because I know how much he is missing. But there is no question that he is learning. He is following an uphill graph. His individual needs keep us from a lot of experience most of the time, but we *have* entered the world of books—though picture books and nursery books they may be, the land of literature has not left us behind. And as usual Will had to remind me of all this. Half the time, it is as if he wants to stop me in the midst of my worrying to say, "Listen, Mom. I'm doing okay."

A week after my library eavesdropping, Will came home from school, wolfed down his after-school snack and stood before me in the living room. "I'm going to read books!" he chirped. Since his reading level had not advanced much past first grade and was a source of frustration for his teachers and his parents, anytime he expressed enthusiasm in the book department everyone jumped to give him affirmation. "Hooray!" I cried. I dropped what I was doing and settled into the couch and waited for him to go to the bookshelf in his room. He came out with a pile of little pink and yellow and lavender books sliding around between his hands. The Tales of Beatrix Potter, his favorite stories of all-time. He'd begun memorizing them at age three and never let go.

He took his place in the chair. "Jeremy Fisher," he announced. He had always thought this story quite hilarious. "Once upon a time there was a frog called Mr. Jeremy Fisher; he lived in a little damp house amongst the buttercups at the edge of a pond." He studied each watercolor as he went along. Jeremy Fisher fished and splashed and got into trouble. Will giggled. "The End!" he shouted and moved on. "The Tale of Peter Rabbit: Once upon a time there were four little rabbits." He couldn't wait to get to the part where Peter escapes mean Mr. McGregor. And so it went for more than an hour, a brisk, lively reading that, though I'd certainly heard it before, held my attention and was thoroughly entertaining. A journey through the pantheon of a different Potter.

He closed the last little cover. "I'm all done!" he grinned. He was so proud of his delivery of this delightful series, and pleased with his attentive mom. There are some strange and big words in those stories—"presently," "macintosh," "camomile"—and Will had pronounced them all beautifully. There is drama, which his passionate narration managed to capture. There is much humor— a fat little kitten whose mother is trying to stuff him into a suit, a frog who thinks he's going out to fish for minnows and instead pulls up Jack Sharp the Stickleback. It is sophisticated, brilliant stuff, actually, as every parent who sits down with it in the nursery is rather surprised to find out. In Will's case, familiarity is all. He loves these stories but he has also gone through each one of them probably two hundred times.

There will be time for the magic of Harry Potter, I realize now. So many things I've pined for have eventually come into Will's life, four or five years late. But these days the story that excites and enchants my still-little one involves a hilarious chase by a crotchety old gardener after a mischievous little rabbit who's lost his way. A huge bestseller, and a classic, world-famous storyline that's rarely been topped.

$\mathcal{I}$nto the Pool

Will can swim. He taught himself, though we tried to get him lessons. He went a few times to a wonderful teacher who worked with him one on one, but one evening he refused to return to his lessons—no big deal, he just didn't want to go back. He stole a few of the techniques he'd gotten from the teacher and created his own style. Now he swims in the deep end with his dad, and he'll even do a couple of laps. He floats. He plunges himself underwater and touches bottom. The minute he hits the pool he is as joyful as I have ever seen him.

Once in his preschool on the University of Washington campus, at the school that was a research site for child psychology, there was a big meeting of all the teachers and therapists to chart Will's progress and contribute suggestions for his improvement. The fact of this meeting amazed me—that without our even requesting a meeting we were going to be able to consult with experts from all sides on the subject of one thing—my child's education and welfare. There was some sort of buzz about one of the psychologists who would be in attendance. He was the big honcho in the Department of Psychology and knew a great deal about kids like Will, but his time was hard to book and everyone told me how excited I should be that he would be a part of the group. When the afternoon arrived, I had my eye on him. I couldn't wait to hear his comments. He listened to everyone talk and said nothing, but I could see that he was really, really listening. At last, after the doctor had heard everything there was to hear about this singular little boy, his turn came to speak. I leaned in toward him. He sat back, stroked his beard, looked at my husband and then at me, and one of his eyebrows went up. "He sounds like a pretty bright little boy and I think I have only one comment. As far as something that might be therapeutic—do you ever take him swimming?"

We hadn't, but we began to. There was a fabulous community pool right in our neighborhood. We thought that maybe the sound of screeching kids might put Will off, but the parents were the ones who, at the very start, needed earplugs. The shrieking sound during Family Swim Time could make for headaches. But none of the racket bothered Will, and as we watched him delight in the water, watched him take to it like a seal pup, it certainly no longer bothered us.

We go to the pool a couple of nights a week. And in the Olympic-sized turquoise pond where dozens of kids splash anonymously, where the wild shouts of swimmers bounce off the tile showers and concrete floors, where boys in goggles wrangle and wrestle each other in water games and beach balls of all colors bob up and down in between them, we are free. Not even the lifeguard notices that we're a little different than the rest. The blessed water lets us blend right in. There may be a moment when, floating on our backs and pretending we are the Wenatchee and the Walla Walla ferries, we stand out. But most of the time we can bump, flap, holler, squeal, be silly, lose our trunks, gurgle, wiggle, and shoot out of the water like rocket ships. No one pays any attention. And Will isn't paying attention to who's who either. I'm the one who really appreciates the anonymity, who looks out over the rippling blue and sees society in its most welcoming form. In Waterworld, everyone is the same.

Plus, the swimming solves a couple of problems for me. One is my resistance to pools, as a survivor of a potential drowning incident; I just sort of never got over a little dunking I had when I was eight. I've had no problem lying next to a pool in the sun of a tropical resort, but you'd never have caught me stuffing clothes in a canvas bag and heading off in the dark to get myself wet. Now, too bad, get over it, I'm there, I'm showering, I'm in and reviving the old breast stroke. Two is this nagging worry I've had about Will and sports. He doesn't do any team stuff. And the rest of the boys are all out there doing it, all the time. But there is life beyond soccer, you know, and we prove it twice a week as we practice and pump away and begin to look more and more professional.

The swim starts at seven in the evening, and Will is at the car door at 6:45. It doesn't matter the weather. On one freezing winter night, the pool heater broke and the water was absolutely frigid. My son dove right in and began darting around like a guppy but I, California-girl-without-the-surfing-credentials that I am, could only stand there with water up to my knees, shaking. I'm sorry, I thought to myself, I don't think I can do this; I wish, I really, really, really wish I were home, right up next to a blazing fire, wrapped in a thermal blanket.

It took the longest time. Standing there like an idiot, at last I did become the object of people's attention. "I can't do it!" I whimpered. A couple of dads looked over and chuckled.

Meanwhile Will, sportsboy, athlete, self-taught slippery sea otter in blue goggles many waves away from me, was fed up. With a huge splatter he blasted himself up from the rippling surface. "Come on, Mama!" he yelled. "Get into the pool!" Once again, the water had liberated him: somehow he was suddenly able to shout out his request, like any regular kid. His spontaneity, so rare, and his sheer ability can on occasion just simply blow me away.

There was no choice but to take a big breath, squinch up my face, and go.

$\mathcal{A}$fternoon on the Piazza

A warm, reassuring hand reaches over into the passenger seat of the car and clutches my own. There's no question: my husband's hand is the thing that gives me strength, that saves me, that is a great comforting gift in the midst of these mutual challenges of our lives. Here we are, holding on tight again on this still autumn afternoon, Charles and me, parked in front of the stately brick building that is Will's elementary school. I can almost hear the hum of little kids learning, sense the shuffle of papers and books from behind the windows of the classrooms, as the fall sun glints off the glass.

Charlie and I have this ritual of readying ourselves to walk bravely into yet another parent-teacher conference, a simple little hand-squeeze, a reminder that we're together in all this. We may be veterans of the scene now, but it is never easy to come face-to-face with the pros to discuss Will's primary education. In the days of his specialized preschool, it was different. The teachers seemed like our close personal friends, and together with them we formed one entity in the service of this terrific kid, feeling as jubilant about Will's progress as we were vigilant about facing his challenges. There was a fantastic feeling of company morale that made you think you were in a Frank Capra movie, since the whole focus of the place was on kids with enormous obstacles in their path.

Public elementary school has been a definite return to reality. The teachers and the principal are our allies, but they sometimes become overwhelmed by the magnitude of their responsibilities—they have so many goals to meet, so many young faces to remember in addition to our precious little one's, and they experience so much frustration. Charles and I sit in the last moments before the gathering trying to summon the strength to walk into the meeting room, because we know we are about to hear some of those frustrations voiced.

This particular meeting, however, began with more friction than we were ready for, and turned out to be one of the worst hours of my life. There were so many problems with Will as he entered third grade—his inability to focus on most subjects, his failure to grasp so many things combined with his stubbornness when he was asked to try to complete even a simple project—that I suppose certain people felt that someone had to be held to blame. Right away his teachers announced to us that as team members we "weren't following through". . . that we were, in various ways, "sabotaging" some of the things they were trying to accomplish. This group of extraordinary women educators —and they are, that is why we have decided our son should be with them—felt that they were having to work beyond their capacity, and they blamed us.

I don't understand even now what the reasons were, but within minutes of the start of the meeting there were tears and high anxiety on both sides. It was them against us, or so it seemed to me in those first moments, and I just couldn't fathom how, with all we had to deal with at home, anyone could think we were a problem. At last I left the room sobbing, determined to jump in the car, drive to Canada, and leave them all there to work it out—the way I often would like to solve all our problems with school. But instead, I wandered the halls while Charles stayed and talked to everyone. He had collected himself after just a few moments of being shaken. He held up our side; I could hear him from the corridor where I was hiding, speaking evenly and convincingly to the group. He ended up being what he has been so many times before—the rock. I was able to go back in with a fistful of Kleenex I'd grabbed from the school office, and by then the climate of the room had changed. It seemed impossible that this meeting was able to continue, to be productive and get back to its focus—the wonderful little boy we all care about. But my husband had saved the day.

That strong hand—I knew there was something in it the first time Charles and I touched. I knew it on the day we married. But how could I know then of all the moments and days to come, when it would be necessary for that hand to rescue me?

❦

Flash back a decade or more to the couple, in their glorious thirties, on honeymoon in Venice. I had started talking Charlie into a trip to Europe when we first met. We were musicians and music teachers and had no money, but he had never been to Paris or to London, and I was determined to take him to the cities I knew and loved. When things started getting serious it came together as a plan in my mind—the H-plan. The ultimate Honeymoon. What a dream it would be, traveling to all the romantic places as newlyweds. London, Paris, Florence, we decided. The Italian Riviera. And Venice.

We somehow pulled together the money it would cost, and, as late spring bloomed across Europe, we actually made the dream come true. There are scrapbooks to prove it. There we are there in Kodacolor: he with tousled hair, in a trendy sport jacket, standing before a dazzling array of flowers on a Paris corner. She, in black sleeveless dress and barefoot, gazing dreamily into the camera from her window perch in a castle overlooking Portofino. At the end of the trip there was Venice. The first night we arrived, we were lost trying to find the restaurant and we ran across a million little bridges, laughing. The sunset and twinkle-lights popped up all around. On the canals, the gondolas were floating past as if ordered there by David Lean. The waiter at the restaurant brought us cannelloni from heaven.

The next morning we found a café and the perfect cappuccino and set off to explore the city. In the afternoon, thundering rains came down, and, with no umbrella, we had to huddle under an awning, freezing in our light spring clothes until it stopped. We hugged each other close, trapped in the doorway of a shop, and Charlie was grumpy. I clung to him and teased him. I sang him rain songs: "Singing in the Rain," "Walking in the Rain," "Come Rain or Come Shine," every song about the rain I could think of until he started to smile. The showers finally stopped and the Italian sun returned in all its glory, warming up the cobbled streets again.

We wandered out onto the Piazza San Marco. The orchestras had just gotten underway. On one side of the plaza, twenty or so white-tuxedoed players and their lively conductor struck up a swing tune. From the other side, a second dance band sent out a waltz. Hundreds of pigeons exploded into the sky and flew past ancient spires, up toward Michelangelo clouds. We were lifted into another era; we suddenly became straw-hatted tourists in some other time. We sat in the sun sipping wine and watching the dancers, enjoying one orchestra and hearing faint horns and piano and drums from the other group across the way. And this is what I remember: Charles got up and took his camera across the square to take a photo of one of the bands. I watched him walk with his confident stride and I sighed like a teenage girl. Mamma mia, I thought, I've married the right guy.

When we got back home, we went round and round about whether or not to become parents. It took a couple of years to decide. In fact, we saw a counselor a few times and it was only after that series of visits with a professional that we could really say to each other that it was what we both wanted. It was a scary decision for us, for we knew the honeymooners would be left behind in the scrapbook, and the scrapbook would close.

When Will was diagnosed and I was falling apart, seeing the world through some sort of tunnel vision for a couple of weeks and having nightmares about my baby's future, Charles said, after a tear or two, "We'll get through this." And we have made it through, as a team. Charles is involved in every aspect of Will's brilliant career, from meetings with his therapists and teachers to helping him do homework to making sure he gets to the swimming pool every week to teaching him to ride a bicycle, and on and on. But it goes beyond the usual dad stuff. He has injected his son with his own sense of humor and fun; he has drawn Will out when Will seemed impenetrable. He has held him and brought him out of his strange, fearful episodes, when his world collapses in a way most of us can't understand, into a place that is safe and reassuring. He lavishes Will with affection whenever they are together. It is stunning to me, when I stop and ponder it, how much he is *there*.

And how unexpectedly it all unfolds. One moment, you and your lover are singing along in bad Italian with Venetians in a crowded bar, to accordion accompaniment on a moonlit night, red wine pouring out of nowhere. And the next minute, the two of you are filling out disability forms for your tiny son.

I once ran across a statistic saying that in families involving a child with special needs there is an 80 percent divorce rate. We steer a rocky ship, my husband and I. We are not always floating on a honeymoon canal. We have had to check in with the therapist, sometimes once a year, sometimes once a week. We've experienced a hard distance between one another from time to time, as Will in all his complexity takes over every spare second of our lives. We have hung on, though. Our hearts are bonded by something that goes even deeper than love.

∽

I have shown William our photos of the Italian trip, and of Paris and the bustling streets of London. He loves them. He wants to know how you get to those places, how long it takes, which hotels have elevators. And when we turn the page to one particular snapshot, I usually force him to linger for a moment, because it's my favorite picture, the only one taken of Charlie and me together during our European trip, after we actually got up the nerve, using crazy gestures, to ask an Italian hotel owner to snap the photo. The starry-eyed couple sits at a cafe table in the light, with butter-yellow walls behind them, and hanging vines of luminescent green. They are grinning like romantic fools, and his hand covers hers.

Singer

I'm sitting here listening and it is unmistakable. It's a lovely, lilting, lyrical voice I'm hearing. It's a singing voice. It's Will's voice. Yet it's my voice.

It's coming from the bath, as it often does now. His pitch is truer than mine, I notice, and throughout the entire performance his energy and spirit pretty much put to shame the so-called sparkle of his show business mom. Whether it's a Neil Diamond number he learned while listening to the oldies station in the car with his dad (and at this moment it is: "Thank the Lord for the Nighttime"), or a classical choice, like "Waltz of the Flowers" from the Nutcracker Suite (a robust version of which he was caught humming a few times during the holidays), well, what can I say. The guy has the same pleasing tone that helped me coast through many a vocal competition. The guy can sing.

He pumps away, warbling and crooning as the faucet runs, and even though he started singing a year or so ago, I still put down the book I'm reading and cock my ears in disbelief. I can't help but pay serious attention to every nuance, every note. By god. His father and I, both professional musicians, once watched him stand stock still in a little kindergarten chorus during a program for the parents in his first year at public school. He was silent. The other kids all sang brightly, levitating with pride, while Will stood mute, his eyes darting around the room. Every now and then he would jump up and flap. He knew what was going on, he was loving the music. But he could not sing.

Then one evening one year later, he recreated the kindergarten program note-for-note in the tub. He sang every word of every song in perfect tune. During that school performance, a stabbing heart-pain had forced a sob from my throat, when Will could not sing the sweet finale, "Oh What a Beautiful Morning," with the rest of the children. And I cried again from my living room chair when he finally did sing it, in his own good time, twelve months from downbeat, in the bathroom on a beautiful night.

The autism consultant who came to our house heard him vocalizing and said, "They don't usually sing!"

Yet I was exactly Will's age, a little trooper of nine, when I made up my mind that I would be a singer when I grew up. I used to put on my roller skates after school, hit the sidewalk and race around the block as Disney tunes and Shirley Temple songs rose from my kid's heart up into the warm Southern California air. I knew singing would be my life. When I became a mother I desperately needed to feel that my child would have music. But when William was four years old and still not talking, I thought—okay, put that dream away. Get a nice sturdy lock and toss out the key.

Something was too powerful, though, to stay locked away. I showered him with the tunes of my childhood, with songs of the Beatles, with classical and jazz and Broadway melodies. I was in his face from the time he was an infant, and although he couldn't coo back, he got it. He latched onto our CD collection, literally— he was one-and-a-half when he started chewing on the booklets and the jewel cases, and got into a regular habit of spinning the discs on the floor. But he let us play them for him too, as he sat in a mysterious trance in front of the stereo speakers.

As with all the information William struggles to process, who knows how these sounds reached him, how they may have touched him and simmered somewhere deep inside, mixing all together and coming out of him at last? His father is one of the top jazz musicians in our city, and the sound of Papa practicing his upright bass rings through the rooms of our home nightly. My teaching practice brings a parade of voice students into the house and from babyhood Will would giggle at the funny-sounding exercises that floated through the air—ming ming ming, loo loo loo. It is all around, it is everywhere, it is our life. But for so long Will seemed incapable of giving us the gift we dreamed of. Now, recently, we've received shocking reports from his teachers: he was actually caught singing Christmas carols in a new school chorus the other day. There is a band for fourth and fifth graders, and our arts-oriented school principal has suggested that we try starting Will on an instrument. The fantasies that were so fleeting, that seemed so out of this mother's grasp once upon a time, now light on my shoulder and stay for a moment, like amazing little butterflies that I may someday be able to hold in my hand.

All I know is that now the songs pour out of him, out of the soul of a person who can still go very stiff when trying to formulate a request, or an idea, or even a simple greeting. There is a different channel, a magic channel, for his music. The repertoire is diverse. Miles Davis (he sings the trumpet solos). Jimi Hendrix. The best of Rodgers and Hammerstein and the best of Bach. We are way beyond the nursery songs of kindergarten now and exploring the classics, as well as the greatest of twentieth century pop. There is no end to it, and my little singer is in his glory. The first thing he does on waking every day is ask me to sing him a song, which I guarantee he will have down pat in a version of his own by day's end.

Another tub time. A splish and a splash and the voice sounds again. "I've been working on the railroad!" it rejoices. "All the livelong day!!" Still on the edge of her chair, the one-woman audience swoons. And thinks to herself—oh, what a beautiful morning.

Miracle Cure

The mothers in the support group were taking turns talking about their kids. I was looking at a handout that had been passed around, only half-listening to what was being said. Then one of the moms, a sweet person who had been with us only a couple of weeks, uttered something that made me look up from my papers with a jerk. "I look at Toby and I just know he's going to be the first one to be cured!" She pushed her chair back from the table. "I can feel it!" she cried in a burst of emotion. "I can tell by the sparkle in his eye!"

I was stunned. Was it the uncontrolled excitement in her voice? I'd heard that sound before, I'd made it myself, I was perfectly used to the emotional tone of these gatherings. No, it was the word—"cure." It jarred me. I felt the urge to push my chair back and hurry out of the room, to go somewhere quiet and do a long meditation on that word. I wanted to take a walk in the woods with "cure." Even now, long after hearing it, I need to think on it. I don't know if it's my enemy or my friend.

Most of the mothers smiled gently at this woman's remark. Then we moved on to our usual business, the business of what we can do while, I guess, we're waiting for a cure. Our children are in front of us now, our children who must be helped, be loved, and be appreciated in this moment, in this time of no cure, for who they happen to be.

On another day, I came home in the afternoon to find seventeen messages on my answering machine. By the time I got to the eighth or ninth one, I was pushing the fast-forward button. "Secretin"—"Good Morning America"—"secretin"—"on ABC this morning"—"a new drug"—"secretin"—"I thought you'd really want to know"—"a cure". . . breathless voices of good-hearted friends and relatives and neighbors, all trying to tell me about the same thing. Secretin. A miracle drug. A possible cure.

But the only thing that had me shaking my head in amazement as I went through the messages one by one was the thought that what is often said about television—that it is without any doubt the most powerful medium on Planet Earth—must be true. All the material I'd read about children like mine, all the stories and information I'd gathered from the New York Times and National Public Radio and the library and the Internet—none of it, apparently, had reached these callers, the wonderful, well-meaning people in my life. Yet a couple of sound bites and a drama sent straight into their living rooms had. It was a big story—the story of parents who had stumbled upon this drug, secretin, when their son was being treated for something completely unrelated to his autism. The parents watched the little boy make miraculous strides almost immediately. And the compelling tale was crafted by a television newsmag into an even more compelling tale. Later I learned that it had sent practically every mother in my position to the phones. Doctors and pediatricians were flooded with requests for secretin. The miracle drug.

Of course, I was keenly interested, and soon after learned that quick action was being taken to begin tests on the drug, at least here in Seattle at the University of Washington where much of the research on autism takes place. In my city, the testing of secretin on a select group of kids began almost immediately after the TV show, with parents lining up with their children to get in on the program. But I didn't sign Will up, didn't wait on the phone, didn't go sit in the lobby of a clinic like many parents did. I don't know why. I should believe in miracles—I do believe in them. I have already seen them happen in front of my eyes.

But I don't believe there's a cure—yet. And because I am always so positive about Will and everything in his life, people are surprised to hear me reject practically out of hand, with an attitude that must seem cynical, someone's new claim of a miraculous finding. But it's really just that the miracles I've seen have not been overnight cures hyped up by TV, but small advances that come in small steps. This is what is real to me, right here, right now. I do believe in a steady, patient hand over a little hand making it possible for my son to write. I believe in someone—a teacher, a therapist—taking his face between her two palms and refocusing his thoughts, over and over again, to get him to concentrate. I believe in creating silence for him so that he can hear and understand, and in making space for him so that he can see. I already have proof that in giving him a script and a story, in helping him to create pictures in his head so that he has something he can hold on to, he can gain more of a grasp on society as he stumbles through it, and can step by step learn to steady himself. These are the ideas that have made a tremendous difference in Will's education and in his life, and these are the things that have actually changed, for our family, darkness into light.

I believe in medication, too. As a person who is rarely caught taking an aspirin, it took me a very long time to put William on any kind of program, but once his dad and I found a doctor we felt we could really trust, we got him on a drug called Luvox and it has helped lessen Will's anxiety in a noticeable way. He is a much happier guy because of it. I also believe in herbal remedies, and in the newest ideas for dietary changes such as removing wheat and gluten from the food menu, although these things have worked for us to a much lesser degree. I believe in staying tuned, staying open, in connecting with other parents. I continually monitor the debate over children's immunizations—the assertion that these could be a possible cause of autism rings true for me, even though I recall experiencing a vague feeling that Will was "different" in my first moments of knowing him, before he had had any immunization shots at all. But "cure"— I haven't gotten there yet.

And since my husband and I so far haven't discovered a way to make the whole bewildering, inexplicable thing go away completely and forever, what do we do? Do we wait, wish, dream? Yes, always, but not necessarily for one big sweeping stroke of magic that could change our son. Because that is the other question that looms, the question of whether or not we need to see this boy change from the absolutely terrific person he is turning out to be. He has made us so happy, and he has made so many people who know him happy, with his strange brilliance. He is such a valuable citizen, possessing so many unusual gifts. As much as I want him to fit in to the world and for the world to treat him well, I also want the world to see that he is, even with his disability and often because of it, a treasure. This may be wishing for the impossible, but it may be what rumbles at the bottom of my heart when someone suggests that he might somehow need to be "fixed." Let the research go on, let us find new ways of making life better, let medicine's advances obliterate the term "autism" from its journals, but meanwhile, here is Will, shining, and certainly not disabled in one very important way: he can teach us so much.

For myself, I register the little, sometimes tiny, strokes of magic. I document them for my own personal news magazine. I thrill to them and I weep. I see them as steps forward, even if they come in painful slow-motion and are way off the mark according to society's timeline.

When I get word of a little pill that I feel certain will give my child a better life, I will be shouting and hanging from the rafters of the support group meeting room. My cry will be heard across town. Meanwhile, the secretin tests, as of yet, have not revealed any successful statistics. The jury is out. But this past year I enrolled my son in a new summer camp where the director, Daniel, who took a great interest in William and had a talent for communicating with such children, happened to be a kind of miracle worker. During the previous summer, Will had been refusing to go on any field trips during camp. It had become easy for him to opt out, to stay behind, and his parents were starting to feel very depressed, knowing how capable Will is of having fun once he's in participation mode, but helplessly unable to get him to budge from his hiding place. He had been spending his bright summer days basically doing nothing. On the third day of this camp, when I came to pick Will up, Daniel came out to greet me. "We had extra seats on the bus for the trip to the farm," he told me. "When I asked the kids who wanted to go, guess who raised his hand and shouted 'I do!'?" This was the first time in my life I had ever heard of a certain person spontaneously raising his hand, without a prompt, all on his own. Daniel, in some way I may never understand, created the magic comfort zone. And guess who went on the trip, petted the farm animals, enjoyed a popsicle, and actually told me later he'd "had a blast"?

It may not have made the evening news. But it *was* a miracle.

*F*riends

I had a goal growing up, and the goal was to find a friend.

For some reason I couldn't find any for years. Maybe it was the fact that I was an only child who was moved around by my parents eight or nine times before I reached the age of seven. There was a pivotal moment in my first grade class, a class I was a part of for only a couple of months before we moved again, which is etched in my mind. The LA sun beat down on the playground. I had managed to luck out, and cute blonde Debbie with the nice dresses had allowed me to attach myself to her. I knew I'd scored. We were walking arm-in-arm across the blacktop at recess, long ponytails bouncing. A boy called out in a singsong voice, "Deb-bie's pret-ty, Kel-ly's pret-ty!" Debbie and I skipped away, laughing. Did I know Debbie for a day, a week? Yet I can still see her blonde hair, her face, her fresh blue-and-white-checked blouse.

And I remember that very soon after that day my parents announced we were moving to Oregon.

I felt like I was standing on shaky ground every time I entered a new school situation, and I entered a new one with the turn of every semester. Shyness wrapped around me like a straitjacket. I was, I now realize, hurting with loneliness. And to make things worse, I was completely uncoordinated. In each new grade, as soon as I tapped the tetherball or tried awkwardly to kick the kickball, my reputation in school spread as quickly as wildfire. I was the Cootie Bug.

In third grade, we settled for good back in Los Angeles, but it took me four more years to hit the jackpot. Her name was Bonnie and we met in seventh-grade math class. Suddenly, by accident, I had magic back in my life. We had the Beatles, old movies from the Thirties and Forties, clothes, boys, everything in common. Bonnie, far more savvy than me in the land of friend-getting, helped us devise a plan to capture kindred spirit Linda, and soon, with the addition of Kathy and Francie, it was a gang of five. A life-changing chain reaction had begun out of nowhere and I came into a completely new world, a place where I began to understand that I could actually own a bit of power. No more Cootie; I was loved. I could walk the halls of middle school with protection and pride. The Gang of Five is now, thirty-five years later, spread out around the world, and four of us are still in close contact. All the confidence I have in the universe came from them.

Life became infinitely easier once I had friendship. But I can remember thirsting for it, dreaming of it, praying for it with all my might before it came.

Now the course of my life has taken me backwards. Back to the praying and the longing. Back to experiencing the isolation that stings so sharply. For here I am with William, a little person straitjacketed himself by a condition that is guaranteed to shut him out of the society of others; the social hardwiring simply isn't there, as one of his docs once told me. He is ten years old, and he hasn't got a friend. It is as if he doesn't notice his peer group. When forced into looking at them, he has no idea what to say or what to do. He must be programmed and prompted to play with them, and reprogrammed with each new kid. And this, of course, is hard on the other kid, who soon gives up on Will. I stand in the corner with him, remembering.

But our struggle is so much bigger than mine was, and all around our house you will see signs of it. A Polaroid tacked to the kitchen bulletin board shows Will sitting stiffly at a table in a therapy room across from another little boy. The caption, written in magic marker by the therapist, says, "Will and Kevin are just right." This photo came from a six-week course in how to have a conversation. Because all four kids in this special class had a tendency to move right up close into the other person's face when trying to communicate, they spent an hour learning just how far apart they should be from one another when talking. Pull out one of our desk drawers and you are likely to see notes in computer print from other sessions. "What do I do when I see someone I know? a) run away b) hide behind Mom c) say 'Hello'."

I had trouble making friends as a child. But with Will's life, we are always starting over, again and again, with the very basics.

The truth of it all is that once more, the pain belongs to me. I think—I believe—that Will doesn't notice that he is lacking, that his life is missing the gift that most kids have, just by nature, happened upon. Due to his intense early education and the commitment and love of the adults who surround him, he has learned to communicate freely with his parents and babysitters and aunts and uncles, and he has made great strides. These friends have patience. They will wait 120 seconds for the first words to form from Will's lips. They will answer his repeated questions, and allow him to speak on the same limited subject over and over again, if they feel that it's the only way to get the spark of communication going. There has been reward for him in trying to connect with these grown-up pals, so he has gotten much better, more confident at allowing his personality to come out. So for now, the adults in Will's world, especially his father and me, are his friends.

I watch life go by, with other families' sleepovers and birthday parties and soccer games, and from my own window see childhood unfolding in our kid-happy neighborhood: two toddlers rolling down the street together on their tricycles, balls being bounced back and forth between kindergartners, kites flying, laughter and crying and shouts and the calling out of names—Joshua! Alex! Olivia!

When I was small I used to wait to hear another child say my name, and now I wait for someone to call out for Will. When I'm not waiting I am an activist, finding ways to bring other children into our lives. My attempts at birthday parties for Will have been heroic. He has seemed to want them, and I've done everything in my power to make them happy for him, but when the guests arrive he usually leaves—he walks out the door and sits on the sidewalk, while the others whoop and holler in their paper hats with frosting on their fingers. It happens whether I create a perfect plan to invite a gang or just two willing classmates, whether I leave it up to chance or clear every last tiny detail with the honoree, whether I keep things quiet and calm or let the whole thing explode into the more normal child-driven racket.

We try playdates, too. The ones that take place at our house yield nothing except one antsy little host who wants to quit the whole idea, and one frustrated guest who wishes he had someone to play with. Visits to the homes of other children, planned and prepared for weeks in advance ("This is what the house will look like. . . Here is what we'll say when we come in the door"), don't usually last longer than twenty minutes. Will recoils from his playmate's unpredictable advance. The stimuli of the new place overwhelms him. At first it is as if he wants to go to the kid's house, wants to be able to play, but it soon becomes apparent that he is very uncomfortable. Often the other mother gets involved trying to assist him right alongside me and we come up with all sorts of ideas—toys that will engage him, holding him in our laps and massaging him while he gets used to the environment. But the most valiant attempts end in failure.

There are little moments of progress in his school life. According to the teachers and staff who observe him, he spends his recess time alone, sits by himself at lunch, and takes long bus rides on field trip days without exchanging one word with anyone else on the bus. Yet when he is forced into some social exchanges at school, he seems to delight in them. Often other kids are assigned to help him at his desk. He will sometimes partner with a kid in P.E. Most of these elementary school children who come into contact with him are sweet and kind, and happy to discover that they have what it takes to help William.

Little do they realize that they are giving him an enormous gift—the important peer contact he regularly lacks.

Meanwhile, Will is content to play at home on his own, to pretend he is a ferryboat pushing across the imaginary Puget Sound of our den, with a dock he has meticulously made from blocks and Legos and pillows. He is alone and he is happy, as long as I am nearby. Heaven forbid any brazen child should make an attempt to share in this game. It is a one-man operation.

I'll watch him play, and it will take me a week or so to muster up the energy, but then I'll pick up the phone again. For, while he seems oblivious to other kids, I am always on the case, searching for a match. I find out from Will's teacher which of the other students are sensitive to him, which ones might be helping him in class. There have been quite a few over the years who are intrigued by Will's persona, who think he's "cool," and though they have not ended up as playmates, whenever I find out about them hope rises up in me, hope I can barely contain. At his summer camp last year, I saw Will arm-in-arm with another boy. The boy's name was Roger. I made certain to get Roger's phone number. Maybe Roger needed a friend too. But somehow I never managed to get the two boys back in the same room together. I usually don't give up that easily, but there are times when even I run out of steam, trying to pull the Friendship Train.

And it may end up to be a long haul. When the Gang of Five went their separate ways and I moved from Los Angeles to Seattle, I continued to go after friendship the way other people chase after money. I wanted to be rich with friends. Into my twenties and thirties I was lucky enough to find more treasure. In a way I happened upon it, but in many ways I also made it happen. I know how to be a friend now. There are rules, just like the rules I've had to script for my son. I'm famous these days for my birthday parties overflowing with warm, radiant women—my best friends. The ones who understand that, though I may not always be able to give them everything the friendship needs because I am so busy giving to someone else, I am a true and loyal heart that will always stay that way, having taken a whole childhood to go from empty to full.

People who know my family or who have observed our home life sometimes suggest to me that I let Will have too much control—over his environment and over me. I agree with them. He wants me to watch every pretend ferryboat run and sit next to him while he watches videos; he wants to tell me when I can and can't play music in the house and he wants to tear up our living room and move all the furniture around to build boat docks. But in so many areas of his life he must still stay so far in the background, with no way, yet, to speak for himself. He can't have a simple argument with a buddy over a game, or shout instructions to a teammate on the soccer field. He has no one his size to laugh with. Until he has that one friend who makes him feel he could conquer the world, I let him conquer me a little. Maybe it helps me with thoughts of the past that keep resurfacing when I look at him. I only want him to be able to enjoy, even for a few moments, the sense of beautiful, benign power that it is possible to feel, just by being yourself with another person who cares about you.

The Lunchmaker

Oh so long ago, when I was in my early twenties, I remember reading a fluffy little pop questionnaire in a fashion magazine. It was titled something like, "Who Are You—Really?" and asked a series of questions designed to help all us early-twenties girls figure out what would bring us the most satisfaction in life. Do you like to draw? Are you good at math? One of the questions caused me to ponder, and is the whole reason I even recall this silly little survey. "Are you an appreciator of the arts, of food, of people?" That question took so much pressure off a struggling young woman—it made me feel that maybe I could actually play a role in the big world of Life, just going around appreciating things. To that interview question, the answer was an automatic, enthusiastic "Yes!"

I don't remember how the upside-down-on-the-page results came out, but it doesn't matter now. I've discovered who I really am, though it took longer than I'd have imagined way back then. I have found the title by which I want to be known, the job that fulfills me more than any other ever has or possibly could. I am a Lunchmaker.

That twentysomething girl I once was, that girl who came of age at the beginning of the dawn of feminism—the one who swore she'd never have kids—would never have believed it. She'd have tsked and rolled her eyes in disgust at the thought of packing someone's PB and J every morning of the working week. But it is a long way for a woman from the twenties to the forties, a complicated journey involving many big surprises, and moments of enlightenment (hopefully), and, for some of us, marriage and motherhood. I experienced my first favorite job when I walked down the aisle at age thirty-six: Bride. It was so great to be a Bride, but it was a temp job, lasting only a few hours at the end of a few months of training. Pregnant Person, another good job, turned out to be a relatively short one as well— that's how it felt for me, anyway. The position of Lunchmaker, by contrast, should hold up for quite a few years.

It was on my son's first day of kindergarten that I got my new calling. Before that, William attended a preschool with a short schedule, and the school provided his midmorning treat. Now I was readying him for the big time. The lunchbox had been carefully chosen for size and color (royal blue). The menu was a collaborative creation and easy to decide upon since Will would only eat five or six things, and crackers and peanut butter sandwiches were high on the list. (This is a situation that still exists, as food is another intruder that can be a terrible affront to his senses—he quickly turns his head away from most things offered.) And so it was all set. I rose on the morning of that first day with great pride and excitement. We were headed off into the big world, and as I packed, things fell blissfully into place. The thermos fit in the middle of the box, between the crackers and the sandwich. The napkin lay on top. All items had been checked previously for easy opening, since little fingers were still in the course of being helped by occupational therapy. On the front of the lunch box I had printed perfectly in indelible ink—"Will, Room 2." My heart soared.

Every school day since then, the yellow-and-black chariot has come to carry Will off. This is the little van-sized Special Ed

bus with just a few kids riding and always with an actual bona
fide saint driving. We have fallen in love with our school bus
drivers, our Kathies and Elliotts and Yvonnes, over and over
again, for now we have had four years of throwing our lunch
into our backpack, hiking the whole thing up over our shoulder,
and tromping up the bus steps into our seat. And you can imagine by now how seriously expert I am at the lunchmaking gig.

There is anticipation every day when you have a kid who's
the only challenged one in his class of twenty-six. As I unscrew
the lid on the peanut butter jar, as I pour just the right amount
of juice into the thermos, as I take a break from doing the lunch
and run around to gather clean underwear and socks, I wonder
about the boy's coming day. Once Will's lunch was stolen right
from under his nose, something so easily accomplished by kids
who knew they can get away with it. He could not report it, or
ask for something else to eat. There have been official reports
by the teaching staff of Will being taunted by the other kids
with name-calling and pushing, and unofficial ones—such as
the time a little girl in the hallway ran up to tell me, "I wish the
other kids would stop saying bad things to Will." The teachers
are on the lookout; the students are generally sweet and kind.
But even when questioned at the end of his day, William can't
formulate sentences well enough to tell me anything about
school; or else he refuses to, in his not-so-atypical desire to keep
home separate from the classroom. What goes on there, every
day, that a mother can't know about?

On a few occasions the staff has called me in, wringing their
hands because they don't know what to do with my son, they
don't know how to teach him, they're getting nowhere. And I
have stood before them, helpless, weeping. When the road turns
rocky like this I understand the value of a ritual. I understand
that my preparation of Will's sustenance for the day is almost
like a prayer. I can't jump in and remake his world. I can busy
my hands though, in a regular task designed to please him and
make him feel safe, and somehow in the little moments of doing
it I can feel safe too.

In spite of all the dangers, and of the times when he has
languished in the classroom and seemed somehow unreachable,

William mostly carries himself proudly through his elementary school days. He does extremely well in the math department. With assistance, he has been known to fly through standardized tests. He roller skates in the gym, he goes happily on every field trip, he reads aloud before his class. Every day gets better. I was so filled with joy over his progress one fateful Friday that I decided to do the cute mom thing and write a little note on his lunch napkin and put a piece of candy next to his sandwich. He came home angry, his food uneaten. The surprise presentation had upset him. He was not expecting it.

So I strive to keep it simple and the same, Monday through Friday, morning in, morning out. It is my contribution to Will's large, looming schedule. It's one of the ways we hold it all together. My maternal love seeps into the project with every stroke of the spreading knife, with every careful sealing of every baggie, with the last confident motion that zips the whole thing together. Every morning when I get up I know who I am, really. Every day, with a purpose and gratefulness beyond anything I ever dreamed I could possess, I make my little boy's school lunch.

$\mathcal{B}$ig Talk

I'd thought about the moment for a long time, and on that spring morning the moment suddenly arrived, barely giving me any choice. I was going to have to find the words to tell Will about his differences. I'd been waiting for the day when a miracle would tumble down from heaven on the rays of the sun, when he would suddenly start looking and acting like everyone else and I wouldn't have to tell him anything at all. I wouldn't have to write the speech of my life. But that day hadn't arrived.

We were having fun on the school playground under a cloudless blue sky. Will was playing his "bridge game"—using a walkway on the play structure to recreate every bridge he had ever seen in the state of Washington—and I was settling in happily and comfortably to watch. Then, out of the blue, came the jarring, clanging sound of the school bell. It was supposed to be turned off today, on a Saturday. I know this to be the rule better than anyone else knows it because I make regular phone calls and talk to school officials about when the bells will ring and when they won't. I don't know what went wrong. Of the many things that can take the air out of my kid, harsh-sounding bells that come with no warning are right at the top. When they sound, he goes directly into spasms. He falls apart with fear. He shakes and cries uncontrollably. I rush to hold him with all my might.

I sometimes operate like a kind of machine in these sorts of situations, switching to autopilot to comfort and console and turning off when it's all over. But today I leave my nerve endings exposed, today I feel all the pain—pain from what? a bell!—that there is to be felt. Rage wells up inside me. When Will was diagnosed, a close friend, a parent, asked "Aren't you raging?" I had no anger then, only a mother warrior's keen drive to go further into the jungle to find the beast and either calmly and tidily kill it or find a way through my desperation to befriend and understand it, and talk it into leaving our family territory. But today I feel another native instinct as I sit here on a wooden park bench mentally shaking my fist at the sky. A bell rang and my child went into spasms and fell to the ground in tears. I have had it with all this. It happens all the time, and we are so tired and so weary and we've traveled so far through clinics and therapy rooms and hospitals and special schools to solve this sad mystery— the mystery of the shock and reverberating pain that comes from a school bell, and countless other random sounds and movements of everyday life.

"Honey, honey, honey," I say as I gather him up off the ground. "Come here, come here, let's sit on the bench together and talk about it."

He is sobbing. "Talk about it," he says.

"Well, we weren't expecting the bell were we? The bell was supposed to be turned off and somehow, suddenly, it must have rung by accident!"

"Yeah." Shaking.

"I don't know why it happened, but I am going to call the school and find out."

"When?"

"Tomorrow."

"No tomorrow."

"All right, I'll do it as soon as we get home"—knowing I will have to fake the call since all the schools are closed today. And this ends the standard portion of comforting words and hugs, the part I have down pat. Now my hug becomes tighter, closer. I feel my breath in his tousled hair.

"Will, do you ever wonder why you get so scared when something comes out of the blue, why it upsets you so much?"

He sniffles. "Yeah."

I hesitate. I'm feeling terribly warm. I never wanted to introduce my child to the label someone else created for him. And yet an instinct tells me it may help him, give him something to cling to for a moment. "Do you remember a couple of times when mom was talking to one of your teachers or therapists I've used that word that starts with an 'A'—'autism'?"

"Which teacher?"

"Well, one or two different ones, I've used that special word. That word describes something you may have been born with. You have something inside you that makes you—well, it makes you get a shock when things happen—when they happen unexpectedly." I am tripping over stones on a strange and difficult trail, picking and sidestepping my way through the underbrush.

And now he's still. He has calmed down. He's listening.

"And sometimes when you feel like you're different from the other kids in your class, that's why it is. It's something called autism that the doctors told us about when you were two years old. It is something we work with and we try to help all the time but sometimes it gets hard. Do you feel sometimes that it's hard, and that things are a little bit different for you than for other kids?"

Stillness. "Yeah."

And silence, as I try to imagine where to go next. Maybe I'm all wrong. Maybe I should never have used that word. But an odd rush comes over me. It feels like, with this tentative back-and-forth, we've suddenly crashed through some floodgate. I feel like a jazz musician who is playing a down and sorrowful blues but all at once finds herself improvising on some unexpected soaring riff, filled with release. Has Will known for awhile that he has a problem; has he been waiting for his mom to explain it to him? There is in all this talk something for both of us to hold onto, maybe in this one moment a way to quell the terror, or even rise above it.

"Papa and I are finding ways to help you. We are always finding ways to help you, that's the good thing. That's why you've had so many therapy classes. That's why you have special teachers at school. And some day. . . ." A sigh I've been harboring escapes my throat. "Someday all the horrible parts will go away."

"All the horrible parts will go away," he repeats. He is rapt with attention, so unusual. I wonder if I'm telling the truth or if in my passion to comfort him I have just burst forth with a gigantic lie. But it feels like I am simply imparting my own beliefs. I do believe the horrible parts will go away. That is how I've held on during this roller coaster ride, and I want him to learn how to hold on too.

"Do you understand what I am saying?" He's been listening to me even though he's been protecting his ears with his hands the whole time.

"Yeah." We hug tighter.

"And so we can get up and go home now, now that we've talked about this. We can have some lunch and play inside in our nice cozy home."

"Yeah."

"Are you ready to get up?"

He jumps up and runs as fast as he can to the car, hands still over his ears, and I sprint after him. The sun is growing warmer. We hop quickly through a children's garden where bright green sprouts are coming up in rows from dark, moist soil. We run to our car, away from bells, away from surprises, away from fear.

Early On

*E*scalatorland

Will is turning six, and I'm getting pretty excited about this year's birthday cake. I think I've figured out how to do it: I'll start with a pound cake, and get it angled at a slant somehow, and start carving. Silver food coloring? They must sell it somewhere. And black licorice for the rails, and a new comb to make grooves in the frosting, and, oh yes, a red gumdrop for the emergency button and. . . my god, it's happened. I've gone insane. I've joined my son in Escalatorland.

I was the one, after all, who really got into it when I decided that it was finally time for Will to create his own birthday party idea. In the past I had always been the theme-thruster—pushing Pooh, touting Thomas the Tank Engine, strong-arming Sesame Street, as Will went cheerfully with the flow. Now out of courtesy and respect, I asked him what he wanted and out popped the concept for which neither Hallmark nor Disney could provide any assistance whatsoever: "I would like an Escalator Party," he grinned.

It's interesting to me that I so quickly accepted this vision, considering the fact that I once despised the big rolling monsters. After a lifetime of barely noticing them, they suddenly began to loom large in my parenting life, for they possessed the power to take my child's mind away from anything a kid would normally love. Up and up, hand-in-hand he and I would go, whenever the people-carrying machine appeared before us. Away from the world we'd float: past the F.A.O. Schwartz windows gleaming with day-glo; up, moving by the colorful garden of kiddie books at Barnes and Noble; up, up, into oblivion, leaving behind the ice cream, the popcorn, the clowns and balloons in the Seattle Center Food Circus—all of the wonders of childhood disappearing below as we continued our slow, steady ascent to nowhere.

From the time he was two, nothing could attract Will like the magical motorized staircase. Like Richard Dreyfuss moving toward the mothership as the *Close Encounters* theme chimed, Will would see the shining steps and head for outer space. And I knew that I was riding in the midst of a controversy: should the parents and therapists of these small addicts let them have their fixations and try to use the deified item as a learning tool, as some professionals in the world of autism advise? Or should we force the children, in a different form of therapy, to go cold turkey, and strictly point them in another direction? Kids like mine will take their narrow interests to bizarre extremes; they will so deftly figure out ways to block out the real world. When you find yourself walking through life holding hands with one of them, their single-mindedness takes you by surprise and has you anxiously wondering which way to pull. If I can, I try to yank him away, turn him around, but his determination and rigidity can make this a superhuman task, and there have been many failed attempts.

One day as my son and I stood perched at the top of yet another landing, with Will jumping and flapping as excitedly as a climber who'd reached the summit of Everest, I knelt at his side in desperation. "Will!" I implored in a harsh whisper, gripping his little arm. "There's more to life than escalators!" But he took my hand and stepped on, and by the time we'd arrived at the next floor of that particular department store he was crow-ing to the shoppers at top volume: "There's more to life than escalators! There's more to life than escalators!" And as folks peered over at us with curious expressions, I began to dream of automatic stairs that could lift me through the roof.

Eventually, though, I began to understand their calming effect. When the stress of life becomes too much, as it does each day for Will, wouldn't I myself seek out the hypnotic release of the Pacific Ocean if I saw that it was available in every downtown bank building? Will had found the relaxation method that was perfect in every way. It never changed. It couldn't come at you from left field—like nature, or a human. If there was an up one there was a down one and if there was a down one there was an up one. The symmetry and regularity could only be disrupted in the event of a power outage, or if somebody got their shoestring caught.

So in the most child-centered style of surrender, I literally went along for the ride. Through department stores and office buildings, hotels and hospitals, shopping malls and airports and bus tunnels, we blazed our vertical trail. I tried my best to educate along the way. We noticed skylights above our heads, babies riding with us, numbers and letters that marked our path. But somewhere between floors my pedagogical stance got wiped out. I found myself wondering about the escalator's innards (which we once got to glimpse during a thrilling moment with repairmen at a local hospital), its history (who invented it? In what year?), and its manufacturers (Otis and Haughton are two proud names one often sees engraved at the foot). I imagined the Midwestern escalator factory we might visit one day in a distant burg like Oshkosh or Fargo. I even pictured mother and son getting together to beat a Guinness record—so many escalators in so many days in so many cities. The two of us, weary but grinning for the media, at the last plateau in some supermall in Canada.

And so the birthday cake, a monument to our travels, but, when I come back down to earth, something I suppose I'd rather think of as a milestone to build and leave behind. There's got to be a way for William and his mom to get over this, or at least branch out. I thought of a new title for Will's celebration and it seems to check out OK with him: Things That Go Up and Down.

This way, in addition to the original and amazing cake, we can include yo-yos, bouncing balls, and swings, to the relief of our party guests, no doubt. And perhaps these variations on a theme will one day allow my little guy to see that, like the waves that roll up and hit the sand, like the sun that rises and sets, in the scheme of things, there's more to life than escalators.

Candy

I know why I let the kids take those little chocolate bars and peel the foil away with their tiny, nimble fingers. I know exactly why I allowed them to eagerly pop the candy into their mouths on that bright, blustery morning a few days before Halloween, the morning that now seems so long ago. I never tried to tell myself, or anyone, any differently. I knew why I was doing it, at the moment that I did it.

Will was two. We were enrolled in a little cooperative preschool with a wonderful teacher named Karen Truelove. She was a love, and in our neighborhood she had become somewhat of a legend—to get your kid into Karen's class, where there was a waiting list every fall, was to have your toddler starting his or her education with the best. We were lucky to make it into the little school called Springbrook. It was a painted blue portable box sitting right next to a stream, with a bridge leading over the water to the kids' playground. On the Introduction Night, when I walked up the wooden ramp to the door of the portable and peeked in to get my first glimpse of the classroom, I was charmed: there were rows of little artist's easels, trays of alphabet blocks and jars of play-dough on small tables, and a loft that contained a library of children's books. I felt a fantastic sense of privilege. Will and I went to school every Tuesday morning. On Thursday nights he went with his dad. It seemed like it was going to be perfect.

But things didn't work out as I had hoped. Will wasn't able to be a part of the preschool program. He didn't participate in any of the games or songs; he didn't want any of the playthings. He marveled at an exit sign above the doorway. He ran away from story circle, as far as he could get from the others in the large classroom group (twenty-two little people plus parents). The loft library was his hangout and he huddled there through most of class time. He couldn't sit in his chair during snack; I had to chase him around the room to get food in his mouth. (I was always chasing, chasing and capturing and holding, at Springbrook.) When it was time to go out to the playground he found the tube slide, crawled in and stayed there. No one could get him to come out. The other parents glanced over at us and glanced away. Every Tuesday morning, as it turned out, my heart started filling with dread, and the little songs and stories of nursery school sent me into unidentifiable, silent resentment.

It was in this setting that Karen Truelove and another teacher brought Will's differences to my attention (not that they hadn't already begun to stand out before my own eyes—but the truth was the hardest thing to see). A neurologist was called, the beginning of a life of paperwork and testing and hopes and fallen hopes began. And after the anguish, confusion, and indescribable heartache, there came a deep feeling of relief and understanding, which in the end left me ever grateful to that preschool staff. But all of this took place after the day of the candy.

We had made it through the first two frustrating months of school to the end of October. On the day of my terrible lapse in judgment the class was having their playground time and Will was, as usual, stuck in the tube slide. The wind blew everyone's hair around in the sun.

I wandered over to a trio of two-and-a-half-year-olds cheerfully playing in the gravel. The experience I was going through, of trying so hard to fit in and never being able to find a way, made me look upon other children with awe, as if they were even more magical and wondrous than they actually are. I was attracted to them, like the unpopular girl in school who observes the cool kids. I saw how they communicated with each other, how they handled toys; they all seemed like little geniuses to me. The close day-to-day experience with my own preschooler was so drastically different. For one thing, there was no speech yet. And I would have no luck at all introducing a stuffed animal, a dish of ice cream. My little boy obstinately refused them, refused the fun of life, and was happiest when I handed him a pot lid so that he could spin it for minutes on end on the kitchen floor. He was not interested in much else. I could never seem to sit him down and convince him, yet I tried each day, with every desperate ounce of motherly energy I possessed.

Suddenly there came a happy cry from one of the kids, a little girl who had toddled a few feet away from me, to the edge of the playground. "Look over here!" she called. "Candy!" The two boys at my feet scrambled over to her. "Candy, candy," they cheered. Propped up against a little stone statue of a rocket ship was a Halloween treat bag, sitting in the dirt, a treasure appearing out of nowhere. It was shiny black and orange, it appeared to be untouched, it looked completely and legitimately Hallmark—it looked like fun. In an instant and before I knew it—because I had no idea how fast little children like this could go to work—all three of them were grabbing at it and unwrapping chocolate like crazy. And that was when, for me, things started moving in slow motion. I saw them eating it, I saw their hands getting messy, I saw them fighting over it and laughing and jumping around with glee. It was like a lovely scene from a film, with me playing the mother. And I didn't want to stop them; I wanted to watch them. I wanted to be a part of giving them this joy. I longed, from the deepest part of me, to give it to them. I didn't really think or care how the bag had gotten there. I know I must have been smiling.

The shadow of a frantic mom blocked the light. "What are you doing?" she yelled over the wind, "What's happening here? Where did that bag come from?" It was Halloween, for god's sake, the bag could have come from anywhere. There was a high school right across the street. I was yanked out of my reverie. I was suddenly nauseous with embarrassment.

The kids were herded back to class by some of the other parents. Karen Truelove arrived on the scene and I uttered something like, "They got to it before I could stop them, I'm so sorry, I'm so sorry." My desperate dream of making a little one happy came to an end in a moment shot through with fear. "Go home," said Karen. "I'll call you."

I gathered Will and his things and put him in the car. I looked at him. Oh, how I loved him. I would never want anyone but Will. I knew I could expect to hear from the parents of the children I had been supposedly standing guard over. I knew what they would think of me.

I was at home sitting in a daze when Karen called. "The parents of two of the kids are okay," she told me in a solemn voice on the phone, only an hour after I had left her. She'd gotten on the case right away, trying to calm the parents, calling the playground people and the high school to find out what kind of trick or treat stuff had been officially passed around. Black and orange bags, matching the description of the one I had allowed to be ripped open by the joyful babies, had been offered that morning at the nearby community center. But one father of a little boy was really upset. He wanted to talk with me. He would be calling.

Minutes later the low voice at the end of the line tried to control the emotion behind it, as this father spoke to me of the potential consequences of my actions. I remembered that he and I had once enjoyed a jovial conversation in the classroom, but now the jokes were over. It was still too early to tell if the chocolate had been left by a prankster, if it had been laced with something dangerous, and the dad's tone was understandably unforgiving. "What if my son has to go to emergency? What if he starts coughing up blood? Couldn't you see what you were doing, how dangerous that was?" He asked me question upon question as he got up his nerve, trying to find out from this idiot woman how the bag had been found, how much of the candy was consumed, and why I didn't take it away within seconds of discovering it.

I felt myself groping around for answers like a murder suspect. And from a cavern inside me the one answer I could give him rose up and touched the tip of my tongue, but would go no further. It's because I don't know what it's like to watch a two-year-old anticipate a wonderful surprise, I wanted to say, but there was no way to harness such strange thoughts and make them into a real sentence. It's because I don't know what a little boy like your little boy says when he's filled with delight! It was because I wanted to see. . . I so badly wanted to know, I needed to feel it, to have a moment of being a regular mom! This was my lonely defense. And it marked the essence of my isolation, but there were no words to describe it—then.

Over that night I fretted, and felt like a child myself, one who had been scolded into knowing she'd done something terribly wrong. But like the autumn clouds that day, everything blew over when it turned out the children were all right—even though my own personal storm was soon to begin. The little boy's dad and I never exchanged words after the telephone call, and a few months later, Charles and I took Will out of the preschool and enrolled him in a special school for kids with disabilities. I stayed on to help at Springbrook and fulfill my co-op agreement, however, even though I was certainly no longer obliged to. I continued my job as editor of the newsletter, brought in snacks, helped clean up the room. I watched over the three kids from the playground until June, as they grew and thrived and finished their year in the blue portable by the stream.

$\mathcal{N}$ew Voice

"This is incredible," my voice teacher tells me, her brow knitted. "Maybe for now you should sit on the stool."

It's my first singing lesson in seven years or more. I stopped coming to this quaint house in the north part of Seattle, where my mentor makes little vocal miracles happen, before I got pregnant. Pregnancy and childbirth boldly ushered themselves into my unsuspecting life, and with all that came the bundle of a baby boy who required an unbelievable amount of attention as he grew and grew. No time for music, for my formerly pampered voice. Now I see some light as I emerge from the tunnel, and I feel like it's time to start working again. But I've pretty much lost it. Lost my vocal stamina.

Her expert hands grip my rib cage. "Breathe," she instructs. She sits back down at the piano. "Now: 'Team-o team-o team-o team-o team-o.'" A simple scale. "Team-o.... team-o!" comes the squawk, and after that there's nothing left. The sound is pathetic, the tiny bleat of a newborn lamb. My serious and seasoned coach, who is also a dear friend, cannot contain herself. Suddenly we're both breaking up with laughter.

It's funny now, I guess, but I know how this amusing sound was formed. For one thing, I did not sleep for two years after Will was born. I danced. Danced him around the house at one a.m., two, three, since he never slept longer than a few hours at a stretch. All good singers are highly aware of the importance of rest. Then came the harder times, the crying times. Weeping can take its toll on the vocal cords, though I never knew it before. But now, in the voice studio, I can *feel* it.

After that came several years of intense speech therapy for my son. The whole family was involved. At age three, Will only had one or two words. The therapist told his father and me that we must talk to him all day long. We needed to loudly emphasize every word we uttered in his presence, and when he did come forth with a word, we were told we must repeat it, two, three times. We must read to him at every opportunity. Singing would be good too. These days followed the sleepless days and the crying days—these were the desperate days.

There was a window during which we must get our child to talk, or the window would quietly close and he might never have a voice. I threw myself into the program, of course. "Ka!" the golden-haired toddler would call. "Cat!" I replied. "Cat! Cat!" "Ba!" he cried out. "Book! Book!" All day long, day in, day out. I was automatically saying no to the recording studio jobs and the club dates that used to crowd my calendar. We could barely afford to have me pass up work, but there was a pressing situation at home that now demanded all my time—and my voice. I had a new career of crooning lullabies and nursery songs in addition to my job of talking all the time, and I performed it with more passion and commitment than I had ever poured into any previous gig.

We visited a speech camp for boys with autism, for an appointment with the top speech therapist in Seattle. On our way into the office we passed the kids, average age ten, who were playing on the playground, hammering on chunks of wood, scrawling on the sidewalk with pieces of chalk. These kids were nonverbal. The tap-tap of the hammer was the only sound rising up out of the midst of seven or eight boys playing outside on a summer day. There was something magical and mysterious about it, seeing this bevy of special boys communicating on some other plane. A golden retriever rushed up to William. "Da!' said Will. There was hope.

In the back of my mind I had begun to prepare myself for a life of silence, the silence I had experienced among the boys at the camp. I researched the tools I'd seen them using that day, the sign language, the picture cards. We never put the cards into play, though, because there was a breakthrough. Just before he turned four, Will started to talk.

And that was when my own dreams, my other dreams, started to sail back to me, carried on the sweet notes of my son's new syllables, as the cage door flew open and he started chirping away at last like a wondrous baby bird.

I don't know quite how to explain this history to my teacher and friend, but I don't think I have to—the voice tells all, everything's there in my sad little squeak. You have to start all over again, the squeak tells me. You've given every ounce of vocal energy away to another cause, it croaks. You gave it up. Squawk, squeal. But you can get it back.

I return home from the lesson, run up our front walkway. "Where did you go, Mama?" Will is hanging out on the porch waiting for me. When he says "Mama" it always comes out in a French accent. "Where did you go?" He repeats most of his sentences. "I had a singing lesson!" I reply, clutching my practice tape in my hand. "I missed you Mama!" he says, little Frenchman, as he grabs my arm. " I missed you!"

It's a distant memory: I once regularly stood under hot lights, rhinestone earrings dangling, sequins twinkling, belting the tunes, stretching my arms out Judy Garland-style at the end where the big note comes. Now I am going to start all over again. I may even make a record when I'm ready. My dreams of musical glory have been renewed. I really believe in my heart that anything is possible.

$\mathcal{S}$oul Deep

My dearest closest friend had just gotten the news that she was pregnant. And so her questions for me came rapid-fire over the telephone line—what did you eat, how much weight did you gain, did you do an amnio—all the things her new state of mind and body made her passionately curious about. How euphoric we both were that this time had finally arrived, how mad with glee, chattering excitedly about the new world we were going to share after years of an old friendship. But it was only the start of the interview and already something was beginning to break down, and I knew it had nothing to do with the telephone wires. Right in the middle of her inquiry there came an awkward pause—a space, the dropping of a word, just a momentary lapse. "You did have. . . well, you had your amnio, that's right. . . " The conversation was losing steam.

Though I might have been imagining it, it felt as if all of a sudden we both knew we shouldn't be discussing what I ate and what I did when I was pregnant. That maybe we should just change the subject, and later, without my knowing, she should turn to someone else with her important questions. One of us or both of us was aware in an instant that my pregnancy might not be the one she wanted to look to as an example, and we were already well into this talk before we realized it.

I know this silence, this space. It shows up sometimes when relatives or acquaintances are trying to express their sympathy that my child turned out differently than he might have. Toward the end of their heartfelt little speech there's this uncomfortable moment—is it mine or is it theirs?—and I feel it, and it passes, like something just blew through on a whispery breeze. It comes at the close of my monthly support-group meetings, a certain energy that is palpable, moving around the room; I can hear it though it has no sound, something reverberating in my bones. The social worker is trying to end the meeting, but several mothers are lingering at the table, not moving from their chairs, looking like they don't want to leave. Moments ago there was lively chatter: we may have discussed everything, feeding issues, attempts at discipline, insurance situations, and stress management. But we haven't talked about sorrow—we haven't talked about guilt. We haven't, and we probably never will go to that place that is so silent and so deep, although it may be the most special, fragile thing we have in common with one another. And it doesn't really matter, for in a minute we can brush it away, change the energy, as chairs shuffle and car keys come out of purses and someone volunteers to bring the chocolate chip cookies for next month.

Perhaps we've all been advised by sources close to us: don't go there. I know that's what I was told right off the bat in the first week I was given the news about my two-and-a-half year old son. A few days after the diagnosis, Charles and I were sent by our pediatrician to an occupational therapist who was so sympathetic and sound that it seemed like a good idea to take her advice. "Are you experiencing a whirlwind?" she asked us when we brought Will in for his first visit, to a big room filled with balls and ramps and ropes hanging from the ceiling. "Yes," I answered, "and a certain amount of guilt." She was only the second professional of many we were to see on that first rocky ride through a series of clinics and we were ready to listen when she said, with a hand on my shoulder and great reassuring kindness: "Oh no, no. . . there will be no guilt."

I believed her for a second. In fact, I never had believed in that nasty word. I felt that life was full of surprises, that accidents could happen, and I tried never to place blame on anyone, especially myself. After we received news of Will's autism, everything seemed fairly close to all right as far as understanding my place in the whole complicated picture. I *was* caught up in a whirlwind—a whirlwind of reading, of researching, of networking with teachers and therapists and mothers, of focusing on my baby in a new way and frenziedly trying to meet his needs. I was so preoccupied I didn't have time to reflect. Besides, my research reassured me that autism could occur in children of parents from all walks of life, in children of healthy mothers, mothers of any age. Its origins were a complete mystery, and everyone agreed that no cause had been discovered. This knowledge was nicely in place in my head during the day, when the sun was bright and my baby's eyes were full of laughter and gaiety. Then night fell. While Will was tucked in his crib and darkness crept through the house, that feeling—just tiny pangs of it but pangs nevertheless—lingered at my bedroom door.

And there in the blackness, God only knows how many times I retraced the days of my pregnancy. I was positive I had gone scrupulously by the book. But if there had been a tiny slip here or there, now it stood out in my memory like the bold graphics on a road sign. The day I was raking the garden during my second trimester and I suddenly toppled over onto the lawn like Humpty Dumpty. I called my doctor, who told me everything was fine, that I didn't need to make an appointment. But should I have gone in to see her? It didn't seem like I'd taken that hard of a fall, but should I have done something more? And what about the time I was filling up my car with gas and a droplet of fuel spotted my maternity dress? I was on my way to a luncheon and I didn't have time to go back home and change my clothes. Fumes? Poison? Should mothers-to-be even be pumping their own gas?

And the controversy over early immunization. Only a few sources talked about it then; it was a rumor floating around a couple of websites. But I *had* made the choice to give my baby shots.

Should I have, should I have? Did I? How, why? The questions poured through my mind into the night, followed by fears about my family history—the alcoholism that lurked there, a developmentally delayed cousin I had rarely seen but whose face began to appear regularly in my half-dreams. There was a streak of anxiety running through my husband's side of the family—a relative had once mentioned it, and I began to ponder something I'd read about studies having found a history of anxiety in parents of children with autism. Unbeknownst to Will's father, I started letting him share in the guilt.

All these thoughts, all these emotions, as wild and unsubstantiated as they truly were, layered one upon the other. I fell asleep as a thousand tears fell on my pillow. I told a friend when it was all over that in these beginning days I had cried every night for six months. Why didn't you tell me, why didn't you call me? she begged. But this was a perilous and sinister cavern, guarded so heavily that no loved one would ever be allowed passage through its secret entrance.

Then, somehow, with the light of morning it was over. I was up with my little joyball of a toddler, running after him like any mom, the positive parent going to the wall for her kid. The days were filled with challenges, but what mother didn't have those? Nothing would stop me and very little could get me down. It was only in the silence of the dark when that feeling rolled forward like a wave and no matter what my rational mind tried to do to fend it off, in its power it would take me over.

I saw my counselor, who let me scream and pound the chair and empty out her Kleenex box. I read more, I talked with myself more, I began to see who I was again in darkness or day—Will's mother. I came to accept the magnitude of the mystery of it all. I lived with the monster and although it took awhile, at last I faced it, and in the end I faced it down.

I still know its power, though. And when it pops back around for a moment, I recognize it.

In the speech therapist's lobby the other day I met a young mother and her two sons—a five-year-old boy who had been diagnosed with autism, and his little brother, who was a typically developing toddler. She introduced them as such, and told me their names—Joe, the oldest and Josh, the tiny one. "I always say that Josh came into my life so that I didn't have to feel so guilty about having Joe," she confided, and once again, in the space that came after her remark, for that is the silence that follows me still, my stomach churned. I thought: Where does that leave me, then, and my only child who is so much the same as your Joe?

And so a few haunting pieces remain. I grapple with images in my head, of the women of the 1950s and '60s with children like mine who were called "icebox mothers" by the leading physicians of the time. In their utter innocence, they alone were held responsible for their child's inexplicable disorder and told by professionals to change whatever it was they were doing. So far from me, they weren't permitted the benefit of this society's enlightenment and progress, in the way a number of things are viewed: the disease of autism as well as the role of women and mothers. I can only wonder in awe—how long was the night, how devastating the isolation, for them? Their own doctors officially pronounced them guilty. I cannot imagine what kind of pronouncement came from their own hearts.

I now know a different kind of night. Somehow Will and I have fallen into this routine of lying together in the dark, singing songs and making up funny little jokes until it is time for me to give him a huge, tight hug, wish him sweet dreams, and kiss his cheek before leaving his room and letting him drift off to peaceful slumber. During the telephone discussion with my pregnant friend, I wish I could have found the golden seed of the first sentence to explain to her that this is what it is all about. That this is what her nine months of a healthy regime should yield: a mystery in the dark, a treasure that comes out of nowhere, someone whose warm, breathing skin you can hold so close, but someone for whom you cannot answer; your own child, a complicated, beautiful mystery. And every evening now, for a fleeting moment, I hold this sweet wonder close to my body in the quiet space of darkness, where once, before I really understood the gift that life can bring, I was so afraid to go.

$\mathcal{W}$indow

Once, I had a window on the world, or the world as it could be, if everything were perfect.

Will spent four years in a preschool and kindergarten designed for children with disabilities, part of a cutting-edge research center on the University of Washington campus. It was there that I think I may have received more training than any of the students. I learned how to be strong. I learned compassion. I learned that there is so much more to humanity than I could ever have imagined before it was necessary to enroll my child in this unique institution. A group of brilliant instructors, therapists, college students, psychiatrists, and little children appeared in my life all at once and let me know, each in their way, right off the bat: we know the meaning of the word hope, and the meaning of the word triumph. Let us show you. I was limping under a cloud of sadness at the time, but it really wasn't long before I broke through the fog and started running along their track of one hundred percent positive energy.

The window—a room with one-way glass that allowed parents to view their kids at work and play in the classroom—was a daily part of my experience from the time Will and I first arrived at the school, known as the EEU (Experimental Education Unit). We had been incredibly lucky to find out about the place, which was rather a secret as it turned out—this was before the Internet, before such information for parents became available with the touch of the keyboard. Our doctor mentioned the initials (I immediately imagined a tiny university) during one of our appointments and when I called information to get the number, I found that the school was just four or five minutes away from our house. As soon as he was given an official diagnosis by a neurologist, Will was enrolled.

I remember walking through the portals of the school on the first day, holding the hand of my little son, as the raw breeze of early spring went through my fragile heart. I felt terribly resistant and deeply sad, to be somehow taking my child away from the "normal" world and walking him into a place for kids with serious problems. Yet in the same moment I felt blessedly safe. There were budding trees all around, and a green hill in the back of the school that rolled down to a shining blue waterway. There were hallways decorated with cheerful children's art, and a big play court with red and blue slides and bright green monkey bars, and sand tables and a dozen little tricycles lined up along a steel railing. At one end of the school was a small gym containing an assortment of physical and occupational therapy equipment—swings and ramps, even a mini-trapeze. There was a library for parents, with books you always thought would be for other people and not you, but now you leafed through them, you clung to them. There were meeting rooms, and a social worker's office. The school was quiet. It was a haven. If nothing else, we could hide here for awhile.

Part of the program at the EEU was to mix kids with challenges of all types—Down syndrome, autism, cerebral palsy, and some titles and labels I certainly had never heard of before—with typically developing, or "model" kids. So in fact we weren't hidden from the regular world—we were right in it. The two closest friends I made while there were moms of model kids. We

watched our children with the same anticipation, we acknowl-
edged each kid's achievements with the same high-five. The
model parents saw how hard the special parents' lives were and
tried to help, and the special parents realized that some of the
things their child was going through were not at all different
from kids' of any size or color or developmental level.

Will slid into the schedule with no trouble, and before I
knew it there was a little bus honking at our door, there to
whisk my three-year-old off to his busy day. The first year, his
teacher was a soft-spoken young woman who understood the
parents' anguish and led us gently into our new circle of friends.
The second year, we had an athletic, outgoing blonde dynamo
who challenged us on every level and who knew that Will was
capable of much more than he sometimes showed. At every
turn of the way Will was allowed to, and expected to, contribute and participate. Of course, these teachers had assistants—
many assistants. There were college kids, male and female,
students who adored the children, coming out of the woodwork.
The principal strolled the halls, peeking into the rooms to see
that everything was going according to plan. Children with
behavioral challenges were not left out of the mix at the EEU.
There were some explosive ones who screamed a lot, and others who occasionally needed to be wrestled to the ground. There
was equipment to handle—helmets, wheelchairs, tubes. In spite
of this, the classes traveled in groups on regular field trips
where they experienced the real world. Most of the time it went
without incident. There were inner city kids from low-income
parents, and children from the surrounding upscale neighborhoods. It all happened on a level playing field, because there
was no tuition at the EEU—it was free.

Will learned to read and write during these years, slowly
and simply but miraculously, and he learned a little math. He
learned to keep his balance on the playground and he learned to
tolerate the feel of finger paint and sand and other textures—
sensory integration therapy was a big part of his program. When
he first came to the school, he didn't have whatever the thing is
that motivates a kid to jump up and dance and sing when music
starts to play, but a teacher would pull him up during circle time

every day as the tunes rang out from the boombox, and soon he saw what it was all about. Mainly, he learned not to hide away, lost in spinning a toy on the floor. He held hands with other children. He looked into their eyes and said their names.

By Will's kindergarten year, our family was completely and utterly spoiled. We had become accustomed to regular roundtable meetings focusing on Will and only Will and everything Will was turning out to be and all he was going to need, with therapists, teachers, tutors, and University of Washington honchos from the Department of Child Psychology in attendance. We had a support group and a newsletter featuring articles by mothers and fathers and all sorts of new information. All the parents received daily reports about their children, who were being constantly observed by professionals and by the young, enthusiastic students of the Special Ed teaching program. Better than anything, we could sit in the Observation Room ourselves and watch the class, and our children's progress, for as long as we wanted, often with a teacher joining us. We pretty much knew we had it made.

I was always bringing friends to the window room, knowing how it would blow them away. We'd sit back in our chairs, watching the typical kids help the others, seeing them laugh and sing together. We'd marvel at the challenged kids, who were often at their brilliant best during classroom time. One of my girlfriends was astounded as she brought her face closer to the glass. "You can't tell who's who!" she exclaimed.

My standard line as I escorted visitors down the hallway and back to their parking place under the trees was kind of a showing-off question: "When you look into that classroom, don't you see a perfect world?"

Then came the final ceremony, the break. Tiny kindergartners marched up to the podium in their paper graduation hats and received their diplomas. Some had to be led to the stage. One was pushed up in a wheelchair. One or two whirled around in a daze, tossed their diplomas into the air, and wandered toward the exit. When Will got up he looked out into the audience, proud as a peacock, searching for the faces of his mom and dad and aunt and grandmother who were sitting together and clapping wildly. A little song was played from a kiddie record: "We'll be together, together forever again."

The families went their separate ways, off into the land outside the green-leafed portals, the land that we all knew would have its tough side. Would we ever enjoy such attention, such understanding, or have the luxury of knowing our kids were way more than okay for a whole day again? The EEU even went to great lengths to place children in elementary schools with good programs and good special educators. They did well by William, helping us to find the right "fit." But sometimes these days I'll run into an alumni mother in our local shopping center, or in a park. "I miss the window," we will both say.

And naturally we miss it. We were given a rare chance to watch our kids' lives unfold, as they grew by leaps and bounds, in what seemed to us to be a perfect world.

$\mathcal{H}$ow the King Became the King*

There he sits on his little throne, Cheerios scattered on the table before him, and on the floor below. "I WANT JUICE!" he demands. "Can you say 'please'?" asks his lady-in-waiting—me. "PLEASE!" the shout comes back.

"Please" is how my son, a five-and-a-half year old monarch with an attitude, fools me into believing he has one iota of regard for me in this situation. I set the juice on the table. "JUNGLE CUP!" he cries angrily. Oops. Wrong move. Slave woman brought the juice in the bunny cup.

How did this happen? His preschool teacher warned me early on. "William exhibits a certain—*noncompliance* in the classroom," she reported. "If you let it go it'll be murder later on." Well. Now that Will is in kindergarten I'm wondering how "later on" got to be now, and what happened to my firm commitment to become a large-stick-carrying policewoman before things got out of hand.

* This essay was originally published in *The EEU Connection,* Spring 1997.

I cut myself a small bit of slack actually, because even though I know that any loving parent can fall prey to the whims of his or her diminutive, sweet-cheeked dumpling, my situation may have been somewhat different. Waiting for Will to utter one word in the English language took such a painfully long time that I can almost pinpoint the moment in which I lost control and went the Way of the Wimp. There had been times when I thought he might never say "Mama." Years had gone by during which I believed I'd always have to make every choice for him. His inability to express his preferences—pointing didn't seem to be a part of his repertoire—left him incredibly frustrated, and more so as he approached age three, three and a half. "Eh!" could mean "cookie" or "Eh!" could mean "bath," and the never-ending queries of people within earshot—"What did he say?"—tired me out. Though she tried nobly to interpret the one-syllable squeaks, even Mama, the eternal optimist, had to admit her heart was growing heavy.

Then one day, when he was almost four years old, Will and I were out for a drive together, stopped at a light. "Which way shall we go, Sweetie?"

I chirped to the back seat. Before I could answer myself in the usual way and make the automatic turn in the direction of my choice, a high-pitched voice came back. "There!" it barked, and in the rearview mirror I looked up to see a grin of delight and a small finger pointing. I was stunned. I was dreaming. With my eyes wet and an enormous lump of gratitude in my throat, I made the left turn.

From then on his requests seemed like big miracles, and my desire to reinforce them knew no bounds. Cookies? Yes, yes, here's a whole box! Playground? Yes, darling, we can stay for the whole day! McDonald's?? You can pronounce McDonald's? *McDonald's* you say! And, with an attack of giddiness, I would set my car in the direction of the legendary rainforest-killer.

A dynamo was emerging and right off the bat he had a willing follower. With his newfound power Will became more settled, more cheerful, and even teachers and speech pathologists became victims of his charm. I wasn't the only one. But somehow, for the others, he learned how to be courteous most of the time. He was saving up the outrageous stuff for behind closed doors.

I don't want to give the impression that his father and I haven't set limits. We know it would be wrong to send him out into the world thinking he can squawk orders and mountains will move. Almost every day now we find it necessary to enforce a "Time Out" or two. We don't throw tantrums in the department store. We don't use the neighbor's daffodils as a trampoline. We don't hit our parents in the face.

But taking a stand on unacceptable behavior is one thing. Dealing with this concept that someone forty-eight-and-a-half inches tall controls the entire Western Hemisphere is another. And every now and then when he finds it deep down within himself to say "I love you, Mama," his status, already too high in our household, somehow moves a notch higher.

The Greek chorus echoes in my ears. "You'll pay for it," said Madame Psychic the preschool teacher. "You'll pay for it," said my best friends, who also happen to be supermoms. I'm paying for it. But it can't go on. We can't have a dictatorship around here, it just won't work, I'm going to have to crack down, I shall have to get mean, I must consult my child-rearing books, attend a parenting class. Meanwhile, there he sits on his little throne, and though his pounding fists shake the table he himself seems unshakable.

"I WANT RAISINS! PLEASE!"

He throws his head back with glee, his eyes twinkling, his giggles so infectious they melt my heart. The king can talk. The king can express himself beautifully. The king is alive and well and confident and happy. Here come the raisins. Long live the king.

$\mathcal{I}$ Can't Explain It

I've passed this homeless guy before. Panhandling on the corner of a bustling downtown street, barely protected from the cold concrete by a tattered sleeping bag and some dirty blankets, he makes loud conversation and collects coins in his coffee tin from the people hurrying by. Whenever I've come near him in the past he's shouted out to me, not to ask for anything but just to say hello—he's crusty and hardened, of course, but he's also a sweet, sandy-moustached old geezer who likes to draw attention to himself. "How's it going today?" he'll say to me in a voice crackly from an ancient cough.

Normally I smile and nod in brief but friendly fashion, but normally I'm by myself. Today I have William with me, and as is always the case when we come close to anybody who might throw us a cheerful greeting, I must approach with caution. An unexpected hello from anyone, friend or stranger, could cause Will to explode into a spectacular tantrum, make him dart headlong into oncoming traffic.

Hand in hand, my little boy and I have to walk past the gentleman to get to where our car is parked. Now my antennae tell me there is danger. Instead of a quarter, this afternoon some passerby has apparently handed the guy a sky-blue balloon. As he spots us coming toward him, he seems to be getting ready to hand it to Will. I know that if he makes even so much as a gesture in our direction—especially with this bright, looming prop—there'll be screaming and struggling from Will and we'll cause a scene. But I have a routine; I've become expert at getting out of these things. Just as we pass the fellow and he's saying "Here you go little one!" and the unwanted balloon is floating in our direction, I grab Will's arm to move him quickly toward the car. "Let's go, Will," I say sharply, and over my shoulder with an apologetic glance I call out to the man: "I can't explain it!"

It's my pat cry. It has taken a number of practice sessions and some tough public experience to get the phrase programmed into the computer but now it's there, ready in a click, a little scrap of armor I can use to fend off looks, stares, commentary, or, in this case, a string of expletives as the old gentleman's sweetness turns street-sour. "What?" hollers the guy. "You think I'll contaminate him? Don't want him to come near me? Why you. . . ." and the trail of obscene names he has chosen to describe this uptight overprotective mother trail off into the city air as my son and I make our escape.

Just like my kid's, my instincts have taught me to flee. In the moment of flight, however, I always feel a desperate need to plead my case. If there were time—if there would ever be time after we've run into a classmate of Will's in the park by surprise, for instance, or seen an adored former teacher in the grocery store—I would love to sit down and explain everything I know. I would tell everyone that even though this little person is reacting negatively, it is really the exact opposite of what he wants—truly, he would be thrilled to take a bright blue balloon; he would love to stay and talk with a friend. But one of the characteristics of his unique persona is that he simply can't handle something he didn't expect, didn't know was coming. He wants, craves, and needs predictability. On the afternoon we encountered the old man and the balloon, I would have had to set up a special meeting with the street gent. I'd have needed to get an exact description of the size and color of the balloon, figure out the names of the streets where we would meet, tell the guy what to say and how to hand over the toy, go home and draw some kind of picture and write a story of what was going to happen and how, and, finally, present the story to Will. Even then there would be no knowing how Will would react.

So, yes, I'll tell you all about it if I have the opportunity and the time. And I will go to those lengths, setting up meetings and writing stories—it's a technique I learned a few years ago, and I have used it many times with positive results. But if traffic is whizzing by and Will is on the run and a balloon is looming like a scary ascending monster, I'll have to toss you my well-rehearsed line and run, no matter what you may think of me. And though I may seem angry or upset or a little crazy, I really am, for a moment, only sad. Sad that we can't meet and greet and tip our hats to you as anyone else would be perfectly happy to do under the circumstances.

When Will was an infant, long before I found out he had autism, I would use this same phrase in earnest. I really couldn't explain it: why I couldn't pop him in the car seat and go visit a friend for an afternoon because I knew there would be wailing at every "unexpected" stoplight; why he turned and crawled away when a cute cuddly toy was offered; why a sudden change in direction in the car or even the stroller would upset him to the point of baby hysteria; why he wouldn't touch even a sugar-coated cereal treat or a cookie. ("Offer it to him differently," my friends would suggest. "Put it in a different dish!") And these well-meaning friends—mothers, all of them—could not stop asking questions, giving advice. Maybe if you don't cater to him so much. Maybe he's too insulated, maybe he needs to be in daycare with other children. A grandmotherly figure in his life thought that he might be a genius. When I talked to myself, this was the explanation I chose.

Then at last, when he was singled out by the teacher at his first school, we took him to be diagnosed. I thought I'd get a big document from the brain doctor that I could edit down and use on friends, relatives, everyone who had seemed perplexed by his early behavior. But there was no document. It turned out that his condition was so mysterious that, although studies had been done and strides had been made, little had been discovered so far. Basically, no one knew very much. With whatever information I could gather, I was going to have to write my own script.

And so it happened that as Will's dad and I found ourselves more and more in situations where our son became afraid and out of control in public, I was forced to develop my first speech for the world to hear: "It's autism rearing its ugly head again!" I would recite it with a weary, slightly bitter chuckle when Will fought and flailed in supermarkets, parking lots, hospitals, shopping malls, and in the middle of the sidewalks of our city. As I straddled this tiny tot lying face down on the cement, both of us exposed to the curious or shocked expressions of passersby, someone might ask me what was wrong and I'd look up with a nutty grin, perspiring from wrestling the force of fifty pounds, fighting back tears and hoping that somehow the blunt truth would make it perfectly clear to one and all: "It's autism . . . rearing its ugly head. . .!"

But the A-word rarely managed to get me the attention and assistance I needed. Once a doctor stopped to help, and occasionally a security guard would hustle over and kindly lift Will to a place where he could get himself organized and begin again—after the guard had determined the boy wasn't being beaten. But usually people just glanced at us and rushed past, leaving me with my emotions and the daunting job of trying to calm, calm, calm this hysterical child. My last, pathetic attempt at getting strangers to understand us came during lunch hour on a crowded avenue, after Will had become terrified by some random sight or sound. I was fighting him to the ground to prevent him from running in front of a bus that was barreling down the boulevard. In the blur of activity, I heard a man shout, "Hey lady, stop beating on your kid!" Startled, I braced Will and looked up through the crowd to find whoever had said it. "It's autism. . ." I whimpered to no one, to everyone, as tears streamed down my cheeks and people brushed past us. A woman came over and tapped my shoulder hard. "It's child abuse!" she barked and walked away.

That incident helped to cure me, liberate me. I really no longer cared what people thought. I needed a quick signal, something that would whisk me past the potential judgment like the horn of an engine that speeds through a clanging railroad crossing. Furthermore, I was certain Will didn't need to hear such a stark description of his actions, didn't need to hear that label again, didn't need to be labeled, really—by now I absolutely hated that label. As long as I was going to have to face these situations and get out of them in a hurry, I figured that I might as well wrap my feelings up in a neat little package and go ahead and blurt them out. I would yell them out, scream them out in as brief a moment as possible. I would find a way to say it all without really saying it: It's one of the most hideous disorders a person can have!! Sometimes it's almost impossible to deal with! It has moments when it can't be controlled! But he's really a wonderful child, the sweetest most loving kid there is and we have found our way through everything to make a very happy family!

And now that's the message concealed beneath the surface of my one-sentence shout. My little boy wants a balloon like any other little boy. My little boy loves attention and loves new people and wants to be around them. But here he is, hollering away, struggling in my arms with all the energy of a lightning bolt. I can't explain it.

$\mathcal{D}$esiree

"Everything carries better in a pack." Will is looking out the living room window, gazing out onto the twin maple trees in our front yard.

"Yes, dear."

"Four new tires, one hundred dollars."

"Yes honey."

"Natural Foods."

"Mmm-hmm."

"'No phony lures'—the one with the fish! Those were the signs!" He's giddy, taking himself on a trip down memory lane.

Yes, yes, those were the signs. Or the slogans, on a billboard around the corner from our house, at the intersection where shady neighborhood lanes stream onto a bustling boulevard. Will remembers every line from every ad that went up during the years 1994 through 1996. That was when I had to start reading them to him, though they seemed to send him such a strong message back then that for all I know he may have been reading them himself.

"Weisfield's Jeweler's!" he reminisces. "Do you remember I was afraid of the signs?" Giggles erupt from him. He gets down on the floor and starts to roll around.

Do I remember? I remember it was not at all funny, standing in front of the parenting section in Barnes and Noble wondering where on the shelf existed the self-help tome that was going to get me out of this one.

He was but a one-year-old when it started to happen.

So many times when we were out driving and we rounded the corner toward home, Will would let out a frightened cry. I always thought it was because he didn't want to go back to our house, that he just wanted to keep driving, driving, as he seemed to love to do. When he turned three, the cry changed to "Na! Na!"—at the same place, the same stoplight every time, with me hopelessly straining in the rearview mirror to try to figure out the expression on his face. Then at four he could talk, and he clued me in. "Don't go past the sign!" he wailed. "Don't go past the sign!"

Oh my god. It was so obvious, yet I'd never seen it. This great big bold thing ascending over us on the corner, with letters thirty feet high. But what was the problem? It had a picture of a giant watch on it right now. Awhile back it had the face of a cute doggie, and before that some radio station's call letters. . . .

And then the light bulb flashed on, after years of worry and bafflement and reaching my hand into the back seat to hold his little arm. Every six weeks or so, the billboard would change. There would be a new ad, a different picture, a logo we couldn't see coming. The sign. He wasn't able to predict what the sign was going to be, and at a certain time every month he would get scared, knowing times and dates as he inexplicably does, and knowing the sign was going to change on him.

It was the first of July, and as usual his calendar sense was dead-on. The billboard was going to change any day, I knew— I'd been watching it closely now, estimating, calculating, feeling like a Vegas bookie. Our route was going to take us underneath it. William stood in the doorway, legs steadfast, blond curls shaking in the summer sun. "No go in car," he mumbled in a tiny voice. But we had to go. We had to get over this one; we had to find a way. Although there was another road we could take, this whole thing had been jangling our nerves, both his and mine, for too long.

I tried cookie bribes and M&M bribes even though these measures had no track record of ever working for me. "Do you want me to call The Sign Lady?" I sighed at last, and it came out of nowhere. There wasn't a sign lady that I knew of—this is what mothers naturally do, they make up SuperFairies to make the scary spider go away. But it quickly came to me that if there was a Sign Lady, a goddess of billboards, then I wanted her. I *needed* her. I remembered the name Ackerman from the bottom of the board—of course I remembered every detail of that board, having scrutinized it out of desperation for so many years. I grabbed the Yellow Pages. I found the phone number. What was I going to ask? That a crew come over now and take the whole thing down ASAP? I dialed. "Ackerman, this is Desiree!" chirped a happy voice on the end of the line. I launched into a fast rap that came from a deep place of insanity and carried me along a swift current to another deep place of insanity, knowing all the while that Desiree would think I was a crank caller.

"Oh hi Desiree I know this is going to sound really crazy but my son and I drive past one of your billboard signs almost every day, the one at the corner of Union Bay Place? And he's just little and he has some special challenges and he—he. . . " I looked over at the door where Will was still standing, frozen like a baby deer, with enormous eyes fixed upon me. "Yes?" Desiree urged. She was actually listening to me. Suddenly it felt like I had my beloved family doctor on the phone as I described the onset of symptoms no legitimate physician had ever heard of. ". . . we would like some information! We wondered if you can tell us when the sign is going to change. My little boy gets frightened when it changes. We want to know what's going to— well, I mean, what we need to know is—well, what's going to be on it next!" It was confirmed: I was a bona fide nutcase. But Desiree hadn't hung up.

"Oh my goodness . . . okay," said the sign goddess slowly as she tried to process my inquiry. "I think I understand. We, um, we don't mind giving you that information. Let's see, ah, I'll check my book. Hold on for a minute." This gal might be considered a dependable customer service rep by some but by the time she came back to the phone I knew she was a glorious angel sprouting wings. There was a billboard fairy. I was going to get my kid into the car again.

"This current one is going to change on July fifth," she prophesied. "It will go from the picture of the watch to an ad for a coffee drink with a photo of a cup and big black letters on a red background. Is that what you need to know?" I repeated all this for Will as she was talking. "July fifth . . . coffee . . . black letters . . ." and I wanted a videocam to record his body language as he relaxed, relaxed, relaxed. Where will he take me next, I thought, as I went with him into a blissed-out state. Here we are backstage of the sign rental biz. Yes, this was what we needed to know.

And on that day we got into the car with a new lease on life. Desiree had given Will a fantastic gift—a picture. A picture in his mind of what was coming around that frightening bend in the road. The Rolex would be there for three or four more days and then the new background would be up in all its crimson glory. He still gripped the sides of his car seat in nervous anticipation as we approached the coffee ad. But things gradually got better and better. At the beginning of each month as we got ready to go somewhere, Will would say "Call Desiree?" It was after a few more predictions from her crystal ball that he started to commit the slogans of the ads to memory, and print them out on his white board at home, and even enjoy them, and laugh at the funny ones.

By autumn, Des and I were staunch comrades.

She had interpreted my craziness for what it was—a cry for help. For a moment once a month, her desk job became part of the helping profession. "Oh it's you, Kelly, I knew it!" she would say when I called. "How is Will doing?" He was doing so well that eventually, after eight or nine months, I didn't have to call anymore.

These days he grins at the memory of it. And I recall that time with the same gratitude in my marrow. Oh Des, Des, where are you now? Are you CEO of the Ackerman Billboard Company? Did they give you the promotion you deserved? You'll never know how you saved us. You got us through. You were the Sign Lady.

School Picture

The principal of Will's preschool called me on the phone. "The class photos have come in!" she almost shouted into my answering machine. "You won't believe William! He's grinning, he's looking right into the camera—he looks like an angel!"

This was unusual, the principal actually calling our house. But there was a reason for it. Anyone who knew Will knew that getting a decent "formal" photo of him was something to get excited about, and when I played back the message, I felt a sensation which at the time was just beginning to become familiar to me (whereas months down the line it turned into a part of me, my way of being, my M.O.). My heart would race with excitement over some possible positive development, then hold back and hold on, because in fact in the end the news might not live up to the expectations of a mother whose emotional state hung on whatever the report might be. The heart galloping ahead, then holding its breath, starting, stopping.

But when the picture came home in Will's Barney backpack, it indeed was a prizewinner. The top of his little mop of curly hair shone white-gold in the studio lights. His cheeks were peachy-pink. He was grinning directly into the camera, and the whole effect was angelic. Any parent would have remarked, were it their little sweetheart—gosh, what a great school photo! But for me it was more than that. My spirit now had permission to soar. This was my son—stuck on a stool where normally he'd have wriggled like a puppy, facing a strange photographer which was certainly, for him, a promise of torture—captured in a flash at his best. Calm, smiling out at the world, confident and happy—this was a Kodacolor miracle.

Gazing at this picture reminded me how far we'd come from Will's first try at modeling, which took place the year before, in a "normal" preschool classroom, when I had no idea anything was up with Will, before the pediatrician had delivered the stunning news that there were some serious and profound problems affecting my child. At that photo session, both Will and I were frantic, operating at the absolute edge. The teacher at the school had warned the parents that it would be no picnic to organize this group shot, that there was going to be chaos and crying for sure. But as moms and dads took the hands of wee ones and herded them over to the blue mark on the floor, my kid took off for the exit, shouting hysterically. He pounded and kicked and wailed against the wobbly door as I tried to reassure him, attempted to restrain him, moved to shield my beet-red face from the other parents. There was no way, as there had been no way in many situations before this, to stop him from breaking away. We ran off into the wet February night together.

In those very early days, we were often beating a retreat, in a panic, on the run, tears stinging our faces. Weeks then passed, and we received a copy of the group shot in the mail. The bright assortment of kiddie faces had come together all in a row after we'd slammed the door and left. Each tiny countenance glowed, as cute as a little bug. Here was printed evidence to show that when it came to connecting with others, Will was an outlaw: he does not appear in his first class picture. I showed it to him, and when he saw it he moved his hand over the photograph. "Eh," he said, and I knew what he was trying to say—"School."

Now years have gone by and I still stare with pride and relief and wonder at Will, age three and shining, in his first school picture, standing in a frame at his parents' bedside. This in all the world must be my favorite image. It bears no hint of the struggles leading up to the moment it was frozen in time: no sign of the day his mom, two teachers, and two therapists had to move his toddler's body inch by inch into the school, across a whole parking lot, down a long corridor, and slowly, with much pain all around, into his classroom (because of some terrible mysterious fear that had gripped him and because he could resist with such astonishing strength). It can't show the terror he could and still does experience when a loud, unexpected sound comes out of the blue, and it doesn't give away the secret that, even at three years old, he was speaking only in vowel sounds. Nor does it warn of the challenges to come—walking into a public elementary school classroom, learning to fasten the snaps on a jacket, trying with enormous concentration and frustration to understand the quick pace of a cartoon video, and still needing to summon his courage every time he has to hold his expression in front of the daunting camera light.

This photograph displays my son in one of his great moments, as he beamingly hands over with innocence and ease the kind of gift that, at one time or another, every mother may be privileged to get from her kid. And in that moment, the only thing the mother can see is all future, all joy.

One Dream

$\mathcal{G}$randma

When Will's first two-syllable word came, it was "Grandma."

I was the only one who heard it. We were leaving my mother-in-law Charlotte's house the day after Thanksgiving and I leaned down to button Will's jacket as he stood in the hallway. I said, "We're going to say goodbye to Grandma now." He answered as clearly, cleanly, and crisply as a little English professor (after years of calling her "Ga"): "Grandma!"

This might have been my first clue that a relationship made in heaven was about to get started. It made perfect sense that Will would try to reach out to his beloved Gram. Grandma saw plainly all of Will's difficulties—in communicating, in trying to be with people, even in attempting to sit for a few moments at her table for holiday dinners. Grandma, veteran of the child-rearing wars, could see that Will was very different from any other child she'd had experience with. But Grandma didn't care.

I once found a section entitled "Autism" in the medical encyclopedia that sat on her table near the fireplace (she had enjoyed a long career as a nurse). "Here it is, Mom," I said. "Here are three or four pages about it."

Charlotte glanced over the section for a moment. "Interesting," she said. She never tried to deny Will's illness—I had already talked her ear off on the subject, and, with her keen intelligence, she had soaked up quite a bit of knowledge. But she thought for a moment. "You know, with two highly sensitive artists for parents," she began, "it follows that he would be as sensitive as he is—doesn't it?"

Who was I to argue? It was simpler for her, and she didn't need any fancy diagnostic terms. She grew up in Ohio, in a big old-fashioned painting of a farmhouse with a huge front porch, and an outhouse and pigs that were butchered every season and chickens she and her sisters would chase after. She learned the piano, a talent she had kept using all her life. She went to nursing school and found her career. She met the man of her dreams and they managed to bring up five beautiful kids. They moved out to a gorgeous hunk of wilderness in the Northwest and built their home and there they remained. Life was pretty straight ahead. She is of a certain solid Midwest mentality that her modern-day citified West Coast daughter-in-law just sits and marvels at.

So that is how she prefers to think of William, as her sensitive grandson. And she knows him well. I've seen the two of them walking in the woods that border her log-cabin house. I've seen Will lying lazily in her arms, rocking in the antique chair on her deck in the autumn sun. Not many words pass between them. But when Will is in the vicinity of his grandmother, she showers him with her serenity and her good cheer, and all is right in their world.

He would have had another grandmother, my mother. But my mom died three years before Will was born. I wonder what Kaye would have thought of him, how she would have reacted to him. She had a hard time facing life's tricky realities and she often could face them only after having swiftly downed a few stiff cocktails. She liked to be able to say things were better than they were. In my elementary school years she had picked up and left me, her only child, on a couple of occasions, leaving my dad and me to search for her, sometimes driving hundreds of miles together in the car. She would disappear for weeks at a time without any warning, and my father would sniff around her workplace and her friends, asking questions and looking for clues.

Later I learned from my mother that she had run off with other men, and that her dependence on alcohol, which she battled all her life, had played a part too. I think that from time to time and apartment to apartment she got tired of dealing with me and with her hard life as a waitress married to a bartender. But the bartender was committed to their marriage and relentless in trying to track her down, and when I was eight she returned to the nest for good, vowing never to leave, and thank God it was not too late to repair the damage. We slowly grew close, though we were as opposite as opposite could be. I was quiet and shy like my father. Kaye was feisty, willful, always laughing and charming the pants off anyone who came in contact with her. She was buddies with everyone.

When my mother came home at last, she proved to me over and over again that her love had no boundaries, that I was the center of her universe. But as I entered my teen years, she denied things about me. She couldn't accept that I was not popular in school, not the pretty thing she had been as a young girl. She wanted me to be some model of teenage beauty and loveableness, and I never was there, so I did my best to entertain her with song and dance. This is what comes back to me when I imagine what she might have been like as a grandmother to William. She would have loved him, with the power of the moon and the stars, for that was how her strong, beautiful heart was made, but she would have denied his disease, or sat late into the night with a glass of red wine wondering how she could fix it. Or maybe not.

No one who met Kathleen Bartley Williams ever forgot her. When she died in my arms at age sixty-seven (of a number of causes that I just say add up to "too much life"), neither of us would ever have believed that I was one day going to become the mother of someone myself. Neither would the jillions of people who came to her memorial service, since it was always my "career" she was touting to everyone within earshot, even when the career was flagging in the dust. But now I've brought the boy who would have been her only grandchild into the world, and sometimes I believe it is her descended-from-Irish blood alone that gives me what it takes to cope. In the meantime Kaye, the funster, plays her little joke on me daily. When William gets a mischievous idea in his head, his eyebrow goes up and his upper lip curls in the most enchanting little smile, and he flashes me a look, and though I am the only one who really recognizes it, there is my mother—Will's other Grandma. With the light of her determination in his eye.

So now, with both the granddads gone for years, Grandma Charlotte is the one living grandparent Will has.

One day at her house, Will allowed his grandmother to sit down at the piano and show off her marvelous style. This is the kind of moment that can go either way—the "surprise" of it can, of course, turn Will inside out and make him start hollering for everything to stop. But I think it was the way she slid gently onto the piano bench and tinkled the keys a little to warm up, and asked him softly if it was all right for her to play. She shuffled through her music books and found the song: "Look to the Rainbow" from *Finian's Rainbow*, and as she followed the notes, the melody chimed through the house. In an instant, Will fell quiet, uncharacteristically frozen in a trance. And from that charmed minute on, his grandmother could never get out of performing for him—he asks her to play that song on every holiday, at every visit. Grandma slips into place on the piano bench, her fine silver hair done up in a French twist and her apron still on from the earlier basting of the turkey. In her mid-seventies now, she is still statuesque, elegant-looking, an accomplished musician. There's a big leather chair next to the upright and Will jumps into his seat a few inches from the keyboard. Then the magic of her music fills the air.

With the fire crackling in the big brick fireplace and the lamps turned low, after the clatter of dishes in the kitchen has died down, toward the end of each family holiday now there is a tradition.

"Well, Will, what's your favorite?" Grandma asks.

"Look to the Rainbow!" Will chirps.

And his aunts and uncles gather around. I feel the presence of my own music-loving mother in the room. There's a sweet introduction played by weathered hands to a perfectly captive little boy, and Grandma sings softly all the way to the last refrain:

> *"Look, look, look to the rainbow*
> *Follow the fellow who follows a dream*
> *Follow the fellow*
> *Follow the fellow*
> *Follow the fellow who follows a dream."*

$\mathcal{A}$ Boy Named Colin

The boy came up to his chair at the front of the conference room. He was a tall, lanky teenager, in a white shirt and black pants, and wearing glasses. His mother, an attractive forty-ish woman with swept-up hair and a big smile, brought him a mug of water and took a seat near him in the front row. A hush came over the room.

The support group was gathered on a Tuesday evening as usual, but tonight the room was packed with fifty or more folks, as many parents as I had ever seen there. I had come alone, while Charles watched Will. Everyone involved with this group for parents of kids with autism or Asperger's syndrome had sent a rep, for we had all received a mailer informing us: tonight was the night Colin would speak.

Colin was beginning to be famous in the community. He was in demand as a speaker now, having done a couple of conventions, even one out of town, for the Autism Society. We were probably lucky to get him. And once in his presence we felt more than lucky. We'd spent most of our parenting lives trying to unravel a mystery, piece by piece, moment by moment, one little tug-of-the-heart at a time. Here, in this nondescript hospital meeting room with fluorescent lights over our heads, we wondered nervously if we could find another puzzle piece. We were all here, quiet, waiting. You could hear people's thoughts, really: Is this who my child might turn out to be?

He had no papers, no notes. He sat back in his chair, looking only slightly nervous, and began to talk to us as if we were friends. "My name is Colin," he announced. "I'm seventeen and I go to Fairview High. I'm here to tell you a little bit about myself and about my Asperger's syndrome."

Immediately we were stunned. This handsome, sandy-haired guy could have been a talking head on your evening news. He made perfect eye contact with the audience, his speech was clear as a bell, and within seconds he seemed to warm up to the crowd. His fingers fidgeted a little, and that was all.

He began by going through the story of his school life. And now we did see a trace of the rigidity that would automatically be a major part of his autism spectrum disorder, the intense need for structure his audience was all too familiar with. He was clinging to chronological order. "In first grade—I had some trouble fitting in. In second grade—I moved to another school. In third grade. . ." His story outline provided him with a way to talk to us. But his mother chimed in from her seat nearby. "In other words, elementary school was hell," she told us all. Colin laughed. It was wonderfully obvious in the very opening of his forty-five minute lecture that Mom was his sidekick.

Finding the right education for Colin had been a rough road, according to his story and the additional comments his mother made. A number of schools didn't work out. He had the problems of a child with Asperger syndrome: social deficits that stood in the way of everything. Some processing problems. A need for sameness, for predictability. Now, sitting here, he was able to recount it in his own words. It was amazing.

With much outside therapy he had made it to high school, where he had a couple of friends. They were computer nerds, and mostly they sat side by side, trading off at the screen playing games. He was on the computer every spare minute of his day. He called the "normal" people of the world "NTs"— neurotypicals. The other kids at school, the ones who looked at him curiously—they were all just "NTs." When Colin told us this, we burst into laughter. He grinned, and you knew he was getting into this new life as lecture-circuit jokester for autism.

Then there was a moment when his Asperger's syndrome actually did take over. Colin told us of how he had had to change high schools the previous year. Apparently the old school could not meet his needs. It didn't provide a place for him to "pace" between classes, one of the ways he regrouped during the day, as well as some other accommodations he didn't mention because by the time he was telling this part of his story, tears were rolling down his face, fogging up his glasses. He was trying to explain the difficulty of changing from one school to the other, how he had been put on a new bus route. That devil—change. He tried to talk about it but couldn't finish. In the middle of the miracle of this boy giving a speech to grown-ups, here was something I recognized from my own life with a boy like Colin. He wept, he ached, just thinking about a disruption in his routine. He froze. The room fell completely silent and someone handed Colin a Kleenex. No one knew what would come next, but since we were all used to scooping up our kids and flying out the door on a second's notice and bringing everything to a stop, we were prepared for whatever the next moment might be.

But it was not the end of the story. After a few minutes he worked his way back and carried on as if nothing had happened. He was on a "medication cocktail" he told us, four different drugs that were the result of much experimentation by the leading docs in Seattle. He listened to classical music all the time on his Discman. "Girlfriends?" he repeated, after someone in the audience got up the nerve to ask the thing that in the final question-and-answer period of the meeting lapped at the edge of all our minds. "I do talk to girls sometimes. I just seem to be too busy with my computers. Girls aren't that interesting to me, and I don't think I would be someone who would be that interesting to them." That was it—move on. He really was, I sensed, dying to talk about his computer games. Dying to take us to the brink of boredom with each and every detail about how each and every moment of each and every game transpired. Another trait I would've recognized right away.

I came to the meeting carrying so much stuff with me, and it wasn't in my purse. I brought the hours and hours of worry I'd known, eyeing teenagers on the street or in the mall, with their gangs, their attitudes, their sheer power. I brought all the time I'd put in looking at television, seeing movies, wondering with every single viewing whether my own son, with his sensory-processing difficulties, would ever be able to enjoy such light and sound. I brought gossamer dreams that my kid, a guy with a resistance to all things new, might someday eat pizza or attend a baseball game. I brought the echoes in my head of words Will had uttered in his cheerful innocence: "After college I will probably get married!" I looked at this boy, Colin—no, I didn't look at him, I scrutinized him down to the button on his buttoned-down collar—in the hope of seeing what Will's future would be.

And I was not alone. During the question period everyone had hung breathlessly on every answer. Colin and his mother, several times during his talk, performed the most wonderful duet. "The clothes you see here," he said when someone asked about wardrobe, "are the clothes I wear every day—a white shirt and black jeans." "He's not kidding," she followed. "We have a dozen white shirts and eight pair of black jeans. Easy shopping." She winked at him.

This teenager had triumphed. He was absolutely charming, in his different way. He was unbelievably articulate—he was doing well. The mom and her laugh and her wink, right there in an instant, may have had something to do with all this.

He got up and said goodnight with a yawn and no emotion, having floored us all. A number of parents moved in to get Mom's phone number and email. Colin may have helped some of us dump a few things from our bags full of worries in the conference room that night. All I know is that for some reason I walked out of there feeling remarkably light—an NT on Cloud Nine.

$\mathcal{L}$ighting the Candles

Christmas morning, five a.m. I peek in at Will. He is sprawled out in the dark in his bed, arms and legs akimbo, face pale and peaceful, beautiful full lips still as the moon. There is no hint of the tyrant he has lately been discovered to be, the strutting little boss of our home. In sleep he's a miracle, all innocence and calm.

How hard it is to believe, looking at him in this pose, that only a day or so ago he was lunging at lamps, banging his fists against a table, creating a terrible scene, making his anger loudly known for all the neighbors to hear. I caused it to happen. I tied one sparkling red and green holiday ribbon around the neck of one of our living room lamps. It was too much for him. All the stuff of Christmas—as any parent knows—all adds up to too much stuff. For a kid who is programmed with different software, it can be much worse. Last night, on Christmas Eve, he fell asleep thinking dreamily of Santa, but the week preceding his sugarplum dreams was a nightmare.

I tried to gently introduce the tiny decoration. I sat Will down on the couch. "William," I told him, "ever since you were a baby boy, we've had Christmas decorations." We have hung sparkly things in the past. But somewhere in the last few years Will blew the whistle on it all. "We always put a few ribbons here and there"—I pointed to the exact places I was thinking of hanging them up—"and we always set out the wonderful Christmas cards people send us—all our good friends!—right over there." I point, to the exact, exact place. I thought I was expert at this kind of preparation since I've had an amazing amount of practice at it. I would keep talking and keep pointing for a few days, and then I would whip out the ribbons and the cards.

But no. A few days later Will entered the room and within a fraction of a millisecond he saw the decorations. "No! No no no no!" As I ran around to lamp and tables trying to save my little works of art, he became more agitated as he began pulling down ribbons and cards, and at last I knew the best thing was to simply give it all up. Give up, once again, something that is so important to me and in a quick moment so reprehensible to him, or at least something he feels a desperate urge to take power over.

Everyone has their dream of Christmas, and I'm aware that anyone who has a child living in their home may face a possible meltdown amidst the music and cheer and Santa hysteria. But my fantasy of the holidays never included a wee one knocking over furniture and tearing things off walls. I do have to admit that the choir of caroling angels answered my prayers on a couple of counts—Will loves the idea of Santa, and he adores the Christmas tree. In spite of how he may feel about other stuff being hung around our home, he is enchanted by each and every ornament that twinkles from the tree's fragrant branches. Because it's an unchanging ritual, he has accepted with joy our yearly trip to the tree nursery, and from the time the noble fir arrives in our living room, spends all his time looking at it and fingering the stars and hearts and brilliant balls. From the beginning I sensed that I should be grateful for this surprising gift of Will's delight. And now that the tree is the only holiday item that doesn't hold potential for an explosion (why, I continually wonder), I cherish its presence. I bow to it and consider it holy. Since tradition always looks the same, there are some traditions our family automatically can expect to maintain.

Yet I wish I could tie those ribbons. I long to paint snow-flakes in the window. I feel a need to light candles every evening during Christmastide, and to keep a fire blazing in the fireplace. Why can't I? After exhausting every positive parenting tech-nique, how can you sit down with a child and in a stern voice try to reinforce the appropriate behavior? How do you attempt to strictly discipline him around a picture of a cuddly white bear in a red Santa hat on the front of a Christmas card?

I am very capable, like a high-strung kid myself, of going off and whining and sobbing over this thing that is getting in the way of my holiday fun. But luckily I am the mother and not the kid, and, as Christmases have come and gone, parenthood and my very special son have taught me a thing or two. I think parents have a chance, after an intense training period and af-ter lots and lots of failure, of coming close to genius when there's a situation that involves picking and choosing moments: when to praise, when to discipline, when to just plain stay out of it. I have learned—the hard way, and only occasionally—how to get a grip, and how to stave off feeling sorry for myself.

I move into the dining room as the winter black stretches into daylight, as the chilly Northwest sunrise with its oranges and lavenders and golds sends a glow through every window in our little house. I peer out and see the solstice stars, twinkling from their pastel stations high above. An excited little pajama-clad urchin won't come staggering out for a few hours, and that seems like all the time in the world. I slip the portable compact disc player into the pocket of my fuzzy bathrobe and position the headphones on my ears: a radiant-voiced choir begins its festival of song. One by one, I light the candles, a dozen of them, my favorite tall ones, fat ones, votives, all in white. And while carols ring in my head, sung only for me, there at last is my Christmas house. The fat jolly tree, the candles burning steadily, and sparse walls—without a single satin ribbon or wreath or sprig of holly or greeting card display or extra added attrac-tion—where the shadows can choreograph their dance. One shining moment for me alone, a treasure brought in with the dawn, as the sugarplum boy dreams his dreams a few feet away.

The sun is almost up in all its December glory. I know that in a little while, I'll blow the candles out and leave not a trace of my pleasure. William will be up, greeting the morning with ebullient shouts and leaps as he has on every Christmas morning since he was two. The stage is set for him, and perhaps that is how it should be; he's the little one. I stand in the frosty window and feel Christmas all around me. And I think: Will is my cause for celebration. Will is my reason for joy. He just can't join me right now.

Hero

It was as if I knew the moment would happen before it came. I had a premonition.

As I was taking Will to the car at the end of the school day, his first grade teacher ran up to me. "Kelly! Kelly, I need to tell you something." She put her hand on my shoulder. "The principal will be calling you today. There's been a problem. We found out about a situation with some kids harassing Will. I wanted to talk to you about it right away!"

I had been living in some kind of crystal bubble and now came the sound of shattering glass. I thought, This is it. We're in public school. This is the start of it all.

The children guilty of the harassment had been brought to the principal's office that very day. Three first-grade boys, just little boys. The principal asked them why they'd done it. "Because we knew he wouldn't be able to tell," one of them said.

What had happened was that every time Will went into a stall in the boys' room, the other boys got into the stall and pushed him around. The teacher wasn't sure where he had been touched. It had happened quite a few times. Will wasn't able to lock the stall door. His fingers didn't work that way. He couldn't defend himself with words or anything else. He didn't have even a semblance of the skills to help him defend himself against the boys—who were really just being boys. But the thought of those boys put my heart in a vise.

The following day I met with the principal, Ms. Clark, in her office. We decided that a teacher or an aide would check on Will whenever he went to the bathroom. Ms. Clark thought that Will's teacher should call her students together in a circle, while Will was in a Special Ed room doing one-on-one, for a meeting about "Privacy." The school had conducted such meetings before. We came up with the idea of getting the on-site occupational therapist to help Will learn to operate the lock on the stall door.

This was the strategy, all laid out in serious tones, a way to cope, and I was grateful—deeply grateful—for the quick action and the high level of concern. Yet a selfish little voice inside me was begging—what about me? How do I protect myself? The answer was already growing, in fact, in the form of a shell around my heart. This first incident—or, the first one I knew about— could have turned out to be much worse. We were at an excellent school. So many of the kids were kind and sweet. To try to watch over Will, I would need to check in more often. I would need to communicate more with his teachers. But in order to shield myself from what might be lurking around the next corner of the brick wall of elementary school, middle school, high school—if we made it that far—I imagined I would have to develop a tougher skin.

And another thought closer to the surface was: who had discovered the culprits? A teacher, I assumed—one of the teachers must have walked in while it was happening. No, said the principal, it had been a child. In fact it was another boy from Will's class who had gone to their teacher to tell the story. But as all the names involved with the incident were being kept anonymous, Ms. Clark wished to keep that boy's name a secret as well.

Yet that boy was my salvation, he was my hope. Was it possible that there were first graders in the world with such a strong sense of what was right? Maybe I just didn't know enough about "normal" kids, but I was surprised to find out that a classmate had come to Will's rescue. After the meeting with Ms. Clark I went to peek into Will's room. Who was it? I wanted to send a big bouquet to his door, with a special letter thanking him and his parents too, for raising a son who, so early in life, understood the importance of helping another kid. And more than that, I wanted to express my thanks to them all for giving me a reason to let go of the dreadful, desolate feelings I'd felt at the idea of fending off such cruelty on a regular basis. When I realized that there was a child like this mystery kid in Will's class, I couldn't help but rejoice that empathy could exist even in the heart of a six year old.

Of course, I had a feeling it was Eric. He stood out, with his dark brown doe-eyes and his sensitive manner. Once I saw him try to help Will, try to play with him on the playground. These are the kinds of things that become etched in the heart and memory of a mom like me. He was my first guess, and the right one. I knew his mother from chats in the school hallway, I even had her phone number in my book. When I called, she said, "Yes, it was Eric."

I knew I must sit Will down and talk to him about the incident when what I really wanted was to whisk him off to Fiji for the rest of the school year, where we would run on the beach and crack open coconuts together and decide, maybe, never to return home. "Did the boys hurt you?" "No." Did the boys bother you?" "Yes." "Well, if they do it again, you can tell the teacher. And we will teach you how to close the door on the toilet stall so you can keep them out." I tried to give suggestions, without playing the whole thing up too much, though I wasn't sure I was getting through. He seemed to have survived what had happened without any psychological scars. It had bugged him a little, that was all. But the same boys harassed him again a few weeks later. A teacher who was on the lookout for trouble walked in on the scene. Their parents had been contacted the first time, and now they were contacted again, and I came in for another meeting with Ms. Clark. But I didn't cry in her office as I had the first time. I was able to garner a little more strength as I spoke to her about reinforcing our strategy.

I found Eric in front of the door to class a week or so after the second upset. I stopped him and put my hand on his little shoulder. "Thank you, Eric, thank you so much—I know you came to Will's rescue," I told him. "Oh, yeah!" He looked up at me with huge eyes. "Yeah," he said again.

From his mom, I got hold of Eric's smiling class picture from that year and tacked it to the bulletin board on our refrigerator. And there it remains.

One Dream

I pass through my kitchen and notice a mishmash of photos taped to the refrigerator door. They've been stuck up in the same place forever it seems, and now the corners have yellowed and the tape is coming off. These tattered prints were cut from magazines years ago; they show pictures of beautiful waterfront homes sitting on hillsides, gorgeous rustic dream houses set among misty pines, overlooking lakes, resting over ponds. The houses peek out at me from the crazy fridge-collage of magnetic alphabet letters and PTA reminders and baby photos haphazardly displayed on the white door—as in so many family kitchens, the refrigerator acts as our home's official kiosk. There was once a dream there, in those little clippings. A fantasy that I could taste. The smell of new pine flooring. The scent of smoke from a river rock fireplace. The feel of a lakefront breeze sweeping over a deck where I could stand out in my bathrobe and slippers and breathe in the fragrant morning air. Where I could be silent, listening for the flap and call of Canada geese. I dreamed of homes, of living rooms full of furniture, of gardens of herbs and English roses.

But now I gaze at the pictures and they seem like an obsession from a very faraway time. I have other things on my mind today. I have a different dream. I've forgotten perfect houses, furniture, linen, china, landscaped gardens, the Martha Stewart lifestyle. That was my magazine world. In it my mind was free to travel to quaint European villages and dip my toes in the turquoise waters of the Caribbean. I could extend the vision and imagine myself a supermodel in Armani, relaxing in a tapestry chair. Staring at my refrigerator, I wonder when I ever had time to go to that place. Or the motivation, even.

Oh, I can still travel off to fantasyland every now and again. And I wouldn't have to be dragged hollering and kicking into the real-life version of that fabulous world. But the material dream is no longer the dream I hold high. It isn't the thing that presses me forward, the goal that burns in my heart. Something took over. Something pushed magazine dreams right out of my head.

It's the dream that my son will be happy, and will find a way to move comfortably through this world.

When you have one big overpowering dream, a mother's dream, nothing gets in the way of it. It has top priority at all times. It's as urgent as a baby's cry.

A friend of mine who has amassed many dollars (and who has remained one of the kindest, best people in my life), once told me how he could pick up on people's feelings so easily, how he could tell when they were envious of his money. But could he have guessed my feelings? While we were on a tour of his House Beautiful, a fairyland compound set among acres and acres of forest, his four-year-old boy rushed up to us and asked his dad in a chirp for a quarter. Such a passing moment, such a normal kid-like thing. Because I had never heard such a quick, spontaneous, lucid request from my own child of the same age, my entire body ached with envy. It isn't a bank account, it's a word I'm jealous of: *ease*.

When Will and I enter into a relationship with a new teacher or a therapist or a camp counselor or even a babysitter, that poor unsuspecting individual is viewed as a potential dream-maker. What doors are they capable of unlocking? Do they hold the key to our happiness? Do they have what it takes to open door upon door? My dreams are patient ones, and as it turns out, we have found that magic and that friendship in many people along the way. And they may never know how many seeds they helped plant in our little dream-garden.

Parents of kids like mine, from what I have witnessed in my years of being part of the community, possess a constant high level of concern for their children's ultimate success, or, in some cases, even survival. If our children are in school for the day, we literally can't let go of the idea of what might be happening in the classroom, of what they may or may not be taking in, of how they are responding from hour to hour. If they are in therapy, we spend the time praying that when they emerge from the session they will have come up even a tiny notch in their progress. When we're with them we keep a careful watch, we intervene, we try to stay keenly aware of how much it takes to meet their needs, like the parents of newborns. Or we may guiltily try to give ourselves a break by letting them play a repetitive game off in a corner somewhere, but really we are incapable of giving ourselves a break, for there is always more to try to figure out, so much more to be done. There is always, always more, even when we don't have a clue what it is that we can do.

We reach, we strive, and it's all for one dream.

I go on the Internet and search for parent groups. I follow up on every phone number that people in their kindness pass on to me. I sit on the floor in front of the Special Needs shelf in the mega-bookstore and read every book. Will talks about eventually living in an apartment, so I'm continually saying to him: "When you get your apartment. . . ." "When you get your apartment, you'll need to know how to open a jar. Come on, let's practice." "When you get your apartment you'll have to know how to put your shirt on right-side-out. Here, let's learn!"

Little steps toward the big dream.

These days, out in the country at my mother-in-law's house, I wander down a needle-strewn path overlooking a silvery inlet, and I stand in the breeze and breathe the pine air, watching and listening for the waterfowl. Back at my own house I'm perfectly happy when I can pull together an ersatz magazine outfit from the old clothes in my closet. My husband and I have talks about the long exotic vacation we'll take alone . . . one day. And we're content with our modest home because it is surrounded by a dozen neighbors who care about our son, who know us as a family and support us right down the line. I have everything I need. It's what William needs that interests me, that drives me, now.

The fluffy towels and embroidered quilts and the set of copper pots—I think they are for someone else.

I have a dream so much more complex. I've moved everything else away. I've set everything else aside. My mind needs to be clear, so I can concentrate.

$\mathcal{E}$volution Blues

Mississippi Doggone Whatever-His-Name-Is shouts in a growl from the speakers over our heads. My husband and I hold each other in a teen-like embrace, rocking awkwardly back and forth to the music, moving our heavy feet just a half-inch or so—left, right, left, right. Guitar riffs blare in short bursts, drums pound, and the mirror-ball above us sends rainbow dots circling around the dance hall in the dark. Tiny colored stars race over the yellow plank floor and all around the walls postered with black-and-white pictures of Fred Astaire. "Just to say hello my little darling—do you remember me? Now it's been a great long time, I just wanna let you see," sings Howlin' Memphis or whoever the gruff, soulful voice belongs to. The music, all blues, is fabulous, the sound system is state of the art. The other dancing couples surrounding us seem perfectly comfortable, and this is only the first dance lesson of the eight-week series.

Charles and I, however, have a long way to go.

"Just an eee-zy rock, back and forth, back and forth," calls out Sean, the teacher, also known as "Gator." He wears one of those headphone-microphone devices like Janet Jackson. "This is the basic step. These are baby steps, everybody go ahead and take it slow. We're just going to do this for awhile." Easy for him to say—he's a tall, strapping blond with, it's apparent from the first beat, incredible grace and confidence. Gator has a partner, MaryLee. They are a reputable team. I did a lot of research before we ended up here, shyly swaying under the lights like a boy and girl who've never met before.

Accidentally, I step on Charlie's toe. He hadn't wanted to come this class. I was really living in a dream to think he would ever want to get up in front of people and practice dance moves, no matter how hip the music. Who could blame him? I set it all up as a surprise, believing it would be just the thing to get romance back into our romance-deprived lives. But I had apprehensions myself. In our entire marriage we had danced publicly but once or twice, and those times stood out as being somewhat humiliating—it turned out we were two professional music makers who managed to completely lose our gift of rhythm out on the dance floor.

It had been a quiet ride to the dance studio. "You're sure you want to do this class," he sighed under his breath as we got into the car. I usually have to move mountains to get a babysitter when we need one. Now I'd moved an entire range in order to procure one for eight Tuesdays in a row. "Yes," I said. The rest of the ride was spent in silence.

At the door, Charles began to feel ill. We were moving up in the registration line and had almost reached a beautiful woman, another dance official, whose name tag read "Selah" and who was taking checks at the sign-in table. "My stomach is bothering me," he said to me. I nudged him through the line. "Honey, it's going to be okay," I said.

When I first broke the news that I wanted to enroll us in this cool-sounding dance class with the quirky title "Evolution Blues," I didn't have to go far to remind him that dancing to blues songs was the cornerstone of our courtship. We had been living together in an old apartment building on Roy Street in a trendy neighborhood in Seattle and every Sunday night the local jazz station would play an evening of blues. We stood in the living room window by lamplight and danced. Of course, given our innate problems, you probably couldn't call it dancing. But whatever it was—bumping, shuffling, tripping—it produced the sexiest, most powerful feeling of romance I'd ever known. Neither one of us could possibly forget that it was perhaps the first way we deeply connected with one another.

That was why the light bulb went off when I heard about this class through a friend. Now here we are, on a fairly crowded floor, in front of everyone, feeling exactly like Laurel and Hardy. "Hello, speak to me," cries the blues singer in a storm of passion. "I been wonderin' where can my little darling be? It's been such a great long time, darlin', do you remember me?" The track pulses loudly. MaryLee strides past us—she's got a matching little headpiece like Gator's. "Just relax, you guys," she whispers. She touches my back. Are we that obvious?

Relaxing does not come easily to two people who basically live their lives at home trying to meet the needs of one very demanding little boy. Our evenings consist of lots of repetition, lots of routine. The same conversations, over and over again, dozens of times a night. Will: "The Chelan ferry looks the same as the Kitsap!" Dad: "Yes." Will: "The Tacoma ferry looks the same as the Wenatchee!" Mom: "Yes." The same kid videos we have watched for six years play in the background of our home, for perhaps their two-hundred-and-fiftieth viewing—we have a heck of a time getting him hooked on a new one. Will can go off on his own a little, but not a lot: mostly one of us is entertaining him while the other heads to a different room for a private moment. All of this along with balancing schedules, worrying about school, wondering about the future. This class is one of the first times in ages we've had a chance to be alone together, focusing on something other than our charge. As a couple, as a Fred and Ginger, it would be accurate to say we're a little rusty.

I look around at the other dancers. There are couples in their twenties, and others who are silver-haired. Everyone looks happy. How many are parents, I wonder, with babysitters at home? How many are taking this class as a form of stress management? Charles and I are like all moms and dads, I think: dying for a break in the established program.

"Do you remember me?" Blind Daddy Whoever yells in powerful tones as the song ends. I'm a singer myself and I can't believe I don't recognize the voice of this great artist. But the music has definitely moved both my partner and me to a new place. I feel Charlie's body loosen as we continue to hold each other, getting ready to hear Gator's next directive. "On this next song push your hips together with your partner's in a little grinding motion. And—we're going to try a dip!" comes the teacher's amplified call. My eyes meet my husband's in a look of panic. But then, we break into laughter.

There are times when our son comes home from school and he shows us his math test with a big red "100%" splashed across the top and we glance at each other in a certain way, a glance that is a mixture of surprise, relief, over-the-moon pride, and glowing satisfaction, and only Charles can know what's in my heart, and only I can know his joy.

Or we look at each other as we stifle our individual giggles, as when we saw Will sitting at the dining room table the other night with a white mound covering the sheet of paper in front of him. "What are you doing?" one of us asked. He held up a little glass saltshaker. "I'm salting my homework," he replied, smiling with the familiar raised eyebrow.

But there is another kind of look we've been missing. The one where Charlie's eyes narrow and stare straight into mine. And it is as if we are suddenly on a misty film set with a computerized moon and special effect stars. And music plays. Lately there hasn't been a time or a place, it seems, for that look to come back to us. We once played lovers in the movie, before we became mom and dad, and it's the lovers' look that was somehow deleted from the script. Tonight we had to talk ourselves into climbing the wooden steps that lead to this hidden dancehall in a poorly lit back alley above a restaurant. But now we're caught up in the blues again, like in the old days. We may have finally found the time, and the place.

The lithesome Gator, who also spins the discs, hops up to the DJ booth in the corner of the studio. "We just heard Lightnin'

Hopkins," he announces, "with 'Do You Remember Me Blues.' You're looking good, everyone. Here's Muddy Waters." He must not have been watching the sorry duo in the back. But when the next driving intro rings out over the room, I notice that my suddenly-very-attractive partner and I have a bit more style going. We've got the basic move. I give a nod to the couple next to us. Left, right, left, right, bump, grind, dip. Charles has a smile on his face. I feel like we're back on Roy Street. Maybe this was a good idea, after all.

Over Washington

Beneath us, fields of green roll toward the sparkling sea. We fly rapidly, steadily. Hundreds of feet below, a miniature light-house moves into our bird's-eye view, standing brightly at the end of a spit, amid a cluster of tiny, pristine white buildings. Sailboats are lined up on the water and their pin-sized masts bob in the sun. We sweep and dip and fly forward, and now we're over a city. This is Will's favorite part of the video, as we almost touch the spindle-top of the Space Needle, and are allowed a few seconds to look for landmarks. But in a moment we've sailed past; once again we're looking down on dots of cattle grazing on a patchwork plain.

Is this the perfect entertainment for my kid or what? When I first discovered it one evening on PBS, I was overjoyed. Will has always seen things from above. If you ask him to draw a house— well, forget the windows, the pointed roof and the door, the classic kiddie's sun and rainbow at the top of the picture. Will draws the overhead floor plan of a house, and always has. He is now famous in our family for sketching overhead maps on his dry-erase board—schools, neighborhoods, the insides of ferryboats, playgrounds, malls. They are always perfectly and accurately rendered, like something you'd see on an architect's drawing table. And it makes so much sense. To confront things head-on—well, this is the most unimaginably difficult thing my child has to face in the world. How much easier it is to avoid the confrontation, the intrusion, by lifting oneself up, and over and out, and trying to get at the situation from a completely different angle.

So we fly. I like to turn down the New Age-y piano music and watch in silence, and so does Will, I think. There are no threats to us here, as we move Over Washington, because there is no time—a thing is there and then it's gone. Of course, whereas my son still finds the scenery interesting after repeated showings, I may space out a little here and there. I go on my own journey, a journey of my past.

൦ᕦ

I settled in the Northwest after one day checking out a stack of books from the library in my hometown of L.A. There, in glossy pictures provided by *Sunset* magazine photographers, I saw the same green hills and blue lakes that roll before me in the video. I knew the trees already, from summers with my parents in Oregon. There was nothing like the fragrance of old-growth forest, nothing like the light of god-rays filtering through the hanging moss. Tall pines and snowcapped mountains beckoned. And even though I had a huge dream of making it as a singer in my Hollywood hometown, I couldn't resist the call. I was barely twenty years old, but I knew I had to travel north and put down new roots.

My first stop in Washington was on an island. In many an island cabin, on the wall by the front door, or for sale in the local souvenir shops, there is a framed print of a poem that reads: "If once you have slept on an island, you'll never be quite the same." And it's so true. I didn't last long on my green isle—I was a city girl and Seattle won out in the end—but when the Over Washington videocam lifts me over and through the San Juans, emerald forms floating on a silver sea, I become a sentimental time-traveler.

I did make a career of music in Seattle, as a big fish in a small pond, and it suited me. Music ended up taking me around the world, in fact, so I suppose I finally got to swim in a bigger pool. For years I never gave one thought to having a child. I didn't want any kids, really. I went through my twenties and almost all of my thirties with a plan, basically, to *not* have a baby. I vividly remember once standing at the sink doing the dishes and looking around at my lovely peaceful Seattle house, when the thought that must at some point cross everyone's mind came into my head. Something I'd seen in the newspaper about a disabled child had sparked it. What would happen, I wondered for a split second, if I had a baby and there was something wrong with it? The horror every woman chooses to put right out of her mind. No, I had a nice home and my chosen field of music to fill me up. I didn't have to think about such things. Of course, I hadn't met my husband yet—that part of my tale was yet to unfold.

◌◊

Sailing down the majestic coastline. We glide in silence. At the edge of the ocean we zoom in close on mystical rock formations. The Northwest held so many stories for me. It was my destiny to come here. Now I see it.

◌◊

Will was a golden, curly-haired baby when I used to rock him to the rhythm of a Shawn Colvin song: "I love you baby/I can see you and I/as we fly away together/up to Orion in the sky." Of the hours of music we would listen to, this was our favorite track, and we'd stand in the living room with the stereo turned up. I must have known something about Will's urge to fly, even then. I held him tightly as we waltzed together, and felt

an incredible bonding as we listened to words about soaring together to the stars. "Maybe somewhere in the southern hemi-
sphere/there can be room for all this love/where they've saved a
place for innocence/and what is still mysterious. . . ." I think it
was supposed to be a song about the environment, yet it spoke
to the mother in me so profoundly, as baby and I rocked back
and forth with our eyes closed and his cheeks like the softest
duck-down next to mine.

∾

Now the great River Columbia is glimmering, rolling, and
we can almost touch it. Within minutes we've popped up to
higher heights, and we're looking down upon craggy, frosted
mountain peaks, the ethereal Cascade Range. We move so fast.
Will coasts along, but he's not much for nature. He's waiting
for another city, Spokane maybe, or better yet another cruise
over Seattle, where he can catch one more glimpse of toy-like
white ferries on a sapphire Puget Sound.

"So I'll see you darlin'/Now fly, baby fly/Down across the
Fiji Islands/To where the Seven Sisters cry/Gather all your
dreams and take them somewhere so far out of reach. . . ."

When he was a brand-new bud of possibility, light as a little
package, how we would rock, and dance.

It feels fantastic to be way up here, gliding over the lush
beauty of the state, skimming its surface, soaring effortlessly
above the world. We could stay here forever, but we won't. The
videotape will buzz to an end in the VCR machine. William and
I will land together on the mossy ground. We'll have to handle
the adjustment, deal with the terrain. He seems to have been
born with a natural ability to tell north from south, east from
west. He knows so much; he'll take me where I need to go. We'll
climb the mountains, and follow the winding trail through the
forest, under the ancient, sheltering cedars.

Some Not-So-Final Notes

As this book goes to press, Will is just about to turn eleven years old. The hardest part of writing about him was trying to make sure each step of the way that no one in our family would one day regret that I'd done it. So far, he seems fine with the whole idea, and I have a feeling that as he gets older, his main concern will be that I got the details right—the names of the ferryboats, the slogans on the signs.

But it is important to note that even though his earlier years were plagued with phobias and tantrums, so much of that behavior has lessened to a great degree by now. Whether it is his maturity that has helped the situation or the constant love of the many people who surround him, he has opened up to life in the past couple of years in a way that someone—not me—might have thought would be impossible. He's still got a tough battle, but at this point his teachers, his father, and I feel that we can look forward to more and more changes for the positive.

In school he is assigned a few book reports each year, and during the creation of this book he'd ask me every week when my "report" was going to be done. Now it is done, and someday I hope he knows that it was done out of a dream for him, and done with the most powerful kind of love.

$\mathcal{A}$bout the Author

Kelly Harland is a vocalist, voice teacher and writer living in Seattle. She is on the music faculty of a prestigious arts college and has recorded two CDs of jazz and pop standards, "American Songs" and "Twelve Times Romance." She won F.E.M.A.L.E.'s award for Essay of the Year with "The Rocking Chair," her story about the first months of motherhood. Her greatest pleasure is spending time with her family. Her husband Charles is a jazz bassist who is known as one of the Northwest's premier musicians. Her son Will, currently a racing car video game whiz and math champ, will soon be a fifth-grader in the Seattle School District.